ENERGY IN PERSPECTIVE

ENERGY IN PERSPECTIVE

JERRY B. MARION
University of Maryland

AP

ACADEMIC PRESS
New York San Francisco London
A Subsidiary of Harcourt Brace Jovanovich, Publishers

ACADEMIC PRESS, INC.
111 Fifth Avenue, New York, New York 10003

United Kingdom Edition published by
ACADEMIC PRESS, INC. (LONDON) LTD.
24/28 Oval Road, London NW1

Library of Congress Cataloging in Publication Data

Marion, Jerry B
Energy in perspective.

1. Energy policy–United States. 2. Power resources–United States. I. Title.
HD9502.U52M37 333.7'0973 74-14832
ISBN 0–12–472275–X

PRINTED IN THE UNITED STATES OF AMERICA

In addition to the acknowledgments expressed in the credit lines accompanying illustrations in the text, permission to reproduce the illustration on page 186 from the following source is gratefully acknowledged: J. N. Pitts and R. L. Metcalf, *Advances in Environmental Sciences,* Vol. I. Wiley, New York, 1969.

CONTENTS

Chapter 4 SOURCES OF ENERGY

Chapter 5 NUCLEAR POWER

Chapter 6 THE EFFECTS OF NUCLEAR RADIATIONS

PREFACE

In 1973 we suddenly became aware that we are in the midst of an "energy crisis." The point was brought home dramatically when the Arab countries of the Middle East—one of our important sources of imported petroleum—suspended all shipments of oil to the United States just before the onset of the winter season. This abrupt change in the petroleum supply hastened our awareness of a situation that was already upon us. Even without the Arab embargo on oil shipments, our fuel supplies were not in a healthy condition. Supplies were (and are) dwindling and costs were (and are) rising. Fuel stocks, particularly those of gasoline, fuel oil, and natural gas, are no longer sufficient to permit the extravagant use we have enjoyed in the past. Several inconveniences are already upon us, with predictions of more severe conditions—even hardships—in store. We have experienced shortages in the supplies of gasoline and fuel oil, and have had conservation measures thrust upon us in the form of mandatory fuel allocations. Increased use of air-conditioning equipment during a severe summer heat wave often overtaxes our electrical generating plants and necessitates cutting back the power output, producing a "brownout."

These experiences make it natural to wonder what our prospects are for the future. How long will our fuel supplies hold out? What new possibilities are there for alternate sources of energy? What new technologies are developing that might alleviate our energy problems?

In this book we attempt to place the "energy crisis" in perspective. We will discuss where our energy comes from, what we do with it, and the projections for the future. We will be concerned primarily with the patterns of energy consumption, the fuels required to produce this energy, and the effect that energy usage is having on our environment. We will examine the overall situation and will discuss both the short-term problems and the long-term outlook. We will devote the major attention to questions of fuel supplies and new energy technologies, and not to crisis remedies such as gasoline rationing, reduced speed limits, and fuel oil allocations.

It is not our purpose here to describe the operating characteristics of the many devices that are used to convert the energy content of fuels into useful forms of energy. We will therefore not discuss the details of electrical generating equipment, storage batteries, fuel cells, or solar converters. However, because nuclear power looms as such an important factor in our future energy picture and because some of the problems associated with nuclear power are unique and challenging (and often misunderstood), we have elected to present some of the details of nuclear reactor operations and their effects on Man and his environment.

As we look at the overall energy picture, we immediately see that we are confronted with a formidable problem in analysis. In order to discuss the energy situation, we must engage in an exercise of "futurism." How much energy will we need in the year 2000? In the year 2050? How much fuel can be extracted from the Earth by these dates? What new technologies will be available in 25 or 75 years? Clearly, we do not know the answers to these questions with any degree of certainty. Nevertheless, projections must be made to guide our thinking and our actions. We will discuss some of these estimates and predictions. In doing so, we will use various facts and figures concerning energy consumption, power production, and fuel reserves, as well as projections of future requirements. When reading these sections, it must be understood that none of these figures is precise. The futurism of energy is an uncertain business.

We cannot give here any clear-cut solutions to our energy problems. (Indeed, there *are* no clear-cut solutions to these problems.) The aim is to present a guide to our recent experience with the utilization of energy and to give some indications of both the challenges and the prospects that the future holds. In some cases we will present the worldwide outlook, but generally we will be concerned with the situation in the United States.

It should be noted that this book is intended for use in classroom courses as a text or supplementary text and for individual reading. It is not intended as a sourcebook of new and authoritative data. The figures, estimates, and projections given here are not original; instead, they represent what the author believes to be the most reliable information and the most reasonable projections available at present. In many cases, the published figures have been averaged or have been adjusted to reflect the passage of time since the original publication. Consequently, sources for the material are given only occasionally.

In this limited survey, we cannot give a complete summary of the extensive volume of energy data and projections. With regard to estimates of future energy needs, for example, somewhat different assumptions (different *scenarios*) will, of course, produce different results. In such cases, the intermediate view is presented and only occasionally is mention made of the extreme positions on either side. This book, therefore, represents a kind of average picture of a very complex subject.

Chapter 1
THE ENERGY CRISIS

We often hear the term "energy crisis" used these days. But what *is* the energy crisis? Is the world actually in danger of running out of useful energy? Are we faced with the prospect of darkened cities, curtailed transportation, and no heat for our homes? In reality, the world's energy resources are plentiful. The reserves of coal are sufficient for several hundred years; we receive vast amounts of energy from the Sun; there is a huge and almost untapped reservoir of heat within the Earth; and the supply of nuclear fuels is almost unlimited. Why, then, is there a "crisis" at all?

THE NATURE OF THE CRISIS

Much that has been written or spoken about the energy crisis—especially about the way energy consumption affects the environment—has been influenced by emotion. But if we are to solve our energy problems, it must be through enlightenment, not through wishful thinking. In this review the attempt is made to provide a dispassionate view of the situation. Problem areas are identified and prospects are presented. Some indications are given of the directions in which we must proceed if we are to overcome the crisis.

The energy crisis is a complex series of problems—scientific, technological, social, economic, and political. Many factors conspire to produce a potential (or actual) shortage of energy even though we are surrounded with a plentiful supply. First of all, the demand for energy is increasing at a rapid rate. There are two separate reasons for this. Not only is the world population steadily rising, but the individual (or per capita) demand for products and services is increasing. Affluent nations require more and more energy to maintain or to advance their standards of living. And emerging nations require more and more energy to convert from agricultural to industrial economies. Even agricultural activities demand increasing amounts of energy (for fertilizer production and for mechanized equipment) to meet the world's food requirements. In fact, the world demand for energy is doubling every 15 years or so.

Increased demand for energy is itself not a factor of great concern if there is no shortage of supply. However, there *is* concern over the undesirable side effects brought about by increased usage of energy. The second factor contributing to the energy crisis is, therefore, the adverse effect on the environment due to the extraction, the transportation, and the utilization of our fuel supplies. Efforts are being made to reduce the spoilage of the world we live in by our increased usage of energy. But every such effort, as desirable as it may be, places some kind of restriction on the utilization of energy and makes it more difficult (and more expensive) to supply users with the amounts of energy they require. Moreover, the nature of the restriction itself generally results in an expenditure of energy (as, for example, in the regulations that require strip-mined lands to be restored).

Although we can see around us plentiful supplies of energy, only a small fraction of this energy is in a directly useful form. The rushing waters of a river represent a substantial amount of energy, but this energy becomes available to light our homes only if a hydroelectric plant is constructed on the river. We know that there are huge reserves of petroleum that lie buried beneath the sea only a few miles from many of our coasts. But before this natural petroleum can be used to power our automobiles, it must be located, drilled for, refined, and transported to the local gasoline station. More and more, the conversion of our energy supplies into useful forms is falling behind the pace at which the energy is required. Even before the Middle East embargo on oil shipments, we had experienced some shortages of fuel oil, gasoline, and natural gas. And the "crisis" is very likely to become worse before we see any really significant, long-term improvement.

The next factor is a geographical one. The sources of our most widely used fuels are not usually located near the places where energy is actually needed. Most of our coal, oil, and natural gas must be transported over great distances. For example, some of the richest reserves of oil in the world are located in the Middle East. Oil from the countries in this region is shipped in large quantities by tanker to North America, Europe, and Japan. The expense of transportation adds to the cost of our fuels, and if the demand for oil increases more rapidly than production is increased or new tankers and pipelines are constructed, it may become impossible to move oil in the quantities required.

Geopolitics is a factor that is closely related to the geographical factor. If a nation depends heavily on a fuel that is supplied by another nation, it is always conceivable that a deterioration in the international political situation could suddenly cut off the supply. In early 1973 the United States imported about one-third of the oil that it used; about one-third of these imports were from Arab countries in the Middle East. Because of the easy availability of imported oil and because of the restrictions on the burning of coal, oil has almost completely replaced coal as a fuel in electrical generating plants along the East Coast. Most of the oil used in these plants is imported. The reduction in the amount of imported oil has therefore placed severe burdens on these generating facilities. Fortunately, the United States is not dependent primarily on any single country or region for its imported oil. (Most of our foreign petroleum comes from Venezuela and Canada.) Western European countries and Japan are in a much more vulnerable position: They import nearly 90 percent of their oil from the Middle East and Africa. In the aftermath of the 1973 Middle East War, it became forcefully evident that concerted action by the Arab states in controlling the export of petroleum can be an important weapon in international politics.

Finally, there are several factors of an artificial nature, including various laws and regulations that contribute to the growing problem of supplying energy in the amounts demanded. We recognize the regulations affecting the environment and human safety as necessary and desirable. Other regulations, such as the quotas on oil imports (now suspended, perhaps permanently), are more difficult to understand and appreciate. A few of the artificial factors are as follows:

1. In order to meet the Federal air quality standards regarding the emission of sulfur dioxide fumes, it is no longer possible in many localities to burn coal because of the high sulfur content of certain types of coal. Although coal is our most plentiful chemical fuel, many electrical generating plants have been forced to convert from coal to oil so that sulfur emissions can be held to a minimum. Moreover, the regulations on exhaust emissions from automobiles have forced the introduction of control devices which, although reducing emissions, also decrease the operating efficiency of the engine, with the result that more gasoline is consumed. These regulations have therefore placed an even greater burden on our oil supplies.

2. Coal from deposits that lie near the surface can be stripped off much more easily and inexpensively than coal that has to be extracted from deep mines. Although there exist large quantities of coal in the United States that can be efficiently removed from the Earth by strip-mining techniques, these methods have often despoiled the land to a serious extent. New regulations will require strip-mine operators to devote considerably more effort to reclaim mined land. The result of these regulations is

certain to increase the cost and perhaps will limit the supply of strip-mined coal, our most accessible fuel.

3. The least offensive of our fuels, in terms of the pollution that it produces, is natural gas. Unfortunately, the reserves of this fuel (in terms of the energy content) are far smaller than those of coal. At the present time in the United States, the price that can be charged for natural gas by the driller is limited by government regulation to an artificially low amount. Drillers are therefore reluctant to undertake expensive exploration and deep-well drilling in order to increase the production of natural gas. (It is expected that these controls will be lifted in the near future.) Because of low supplies, most gas companies have stopped expanding their service to new customers and, on occasion, have been forced to curtail service in some areas.

4. Vast amounts of oil are locked in the extensive deposits of shale found in the states of the Northern Plains and in the tar sands of Canada. We now have no practical method for extracting this oil. In spite of the richness of these deposits, and even though a pilot plant has been operated, only very recently has serious attention been given to developing an economical method for adding this oil to our supply.

5. As our supplies of coal, oil, and natural gas dwindle, we must place an increasing emphasis on the use of nuclear fuels in the generation of electrical power. Although nuclear fuels will not be the major source of our electrical power in this century, they will probably become so within 50 to 100 years. As more and more nuclear power plants are planned and built, it has become increasingly difficult to obtain public acceptance for these plants. The result has been a significant slowdown in bringing new generating facilities into operation. During periods of high usage of electrical energy, the existing plants are often called upon to deliver peak capacity. Any failure during a period of small or no reserve capacity means a "brownout" or a "blackout."

In retrospect it seems obvious that we should have begun years ago to address ourselves to the problem of energy supply. But as long as we could flick a switch and have as much electrical energy as we needed, and as long as we could drive to any gasoline station and fill our tanks, there seemed to be no problem at all. With shortages now appearing, we finally realize that there is indeed an "energy crisis." In 1973 we began to take some of the positive steps that are necessary to meet the energy challenge. Research monies are being made available to investigate alternative sources of energy, with the expectation that billions of dollars will be expended during the next few years. The main efforts with regard to conventional fuels will be directed into three areas: (1) the conversion of coal into gaseous and liquid fuels (coal *gasification* and *liquefaction*) in order to eliminate the noxious fumes and smoke that result from the burning process, (2) the extraction of oil from shale deposits, and (3) the removal of a significantly greater fraction of oil from tapped oil deposits (at present an average of only about 30 percent of the oil in a field is actually extracted). In addition, increased research and development will be carried out toward making breeder reactors and fusion reactors operational parts of the energy supply and to investigate alternate sources such as solar and geothermal power.

THE FUTURE—BRIGHT OR BLEAK?

What will our world be like in 1985 or 2000? Will the problems of supplying energy finally have caught up with us? Will the many facets of the energy crisis have proved too much for Mankind to handle? Will we be forced into a worldwide austerity program with regard to energy and, consequently, with regard to our standard of living? Or, will we have solved our energy problems so that we will have inexpensive and plentiful supplies to run a world even more dependent on energy-hungry high technology?

Our problem for the future is twofold. First, we are in no immediate danger of exhausting our supplies of conventional fuels (coal, oil, and natural gas) or of uranium, the primary nuclear fuel at present. But although the natural supplies are still abundant, it is becoming increasingly difficult to extract these fuels from the ground and to deliver them to the consumer in the quantities demanded. Moreover, we must learn to use these fuels in ways that do not seriously degrade our environment. We cannot expect that the mining of coal, the drilling for oil and natural gas, or the burning of these fuels will ever be accomplished with *zero* effect on the environment. Nor will a nuclear fission reactor ever be built that will not produce substantial amounts of potentially dangerous radioactivity. But we can hope that ways will be found to reduce the degradation of our world and its atmosphere to levels that will permit us to continue to enjoy our energy-rich planet.

Second, the long-range problem involves developing new sources of energy. At some time in the future, we *will* have depleted the coal, oil, natural gas, and uranium resources of the world to the point that we can no longer rely on these fuels as major sources of energy. The three primary but so far undeveloped new sources of energy for the future are solar energy, geothermal energy, and nuclear fusion energy. In each case we know in principle how to extract and use the energy, but the technology to do so on a large scale does not now exist. We discuss each of these new energy sources later in this book; briefly, the situation is as follows.

At a few places in the world, hot underground water is piped to the surface and is used to heat homes and to drive electrical generators. Although the amount of heat energy within the Earth—geothermal energy—is truly enormous, we have no idea at present how this energy might be made available on a widespread basis.

Solar energy appears to be somewhat more promising. Various proposals have been made to construct "solar farms," huge arrays of special materials that convert the energy in sunlight into electrical energy. In all schemes to utilize solar energy, we must contend with the fact that the incoming energy at any time is spread over the entire sunlit part of the world and is not concentrated conveniently in any one place. In order to collect sufficient sunlight so that the electrical output is comparable with a conventional power plant, an extremely large area must be covered with sunlight converters. Although we know how to convert solar energy into electrical energy on a small scale (this is routinely done, for example, with solar cells on spacecraft), the technology does not yet exist to utilize solar energy on a large scale.

Probably the brightest hope for the future lies in fusion power. Energy is released whenever two nuclei with small masses are made to fuse together into a single, more massive nucleus. In the ocean waters, there is an almost unlimited supply of deuterium (heavy hydrogen) which, together with the abundant metal lithium, can serve as nuclear fusion fuel. Extremely high temperatures (measured in millions of degrees) are required to force nuclei to undergo fusion. We have not yet been able to discover a way to confine the fuel materials at these temperatures and to extract useful amounts of fusion energy. Substantial progress has been made in understanding the behavior of matter under fusion conditions, and the prospect is that we will have a prototype fusion power plant in operation before the end of this century. If the development of fusion power is in fact successful, we can look forward to the time 50 or so years hence when electrical energy will be produced cheaply and cleanly and will be available on a widespread basis.

We cannot be certain that our hopes for fusion power (or for solar or geothermal energy) will actually be realized. In any event, these new sources cannot be developed in time to alleviate shortages of the type we are now experiencing. At best, these sources represent long-term developments. If the technical problems cannot be solved before we exhaust our supplies of conventional fuels and of uranium for nuclear fission power plants, we will then be faced with an energy crisis of enormous proportions. For this reason, development of an interim or backup energy source is under way in the form of *breeder reactors*. Fission reactors of the type now used in nuclear power plants consume uranium fuel. A breeder reactor is a fission reactor in which nuclear energy is released and at the same time new fuel is produced. Because new fuel can be produced from materials that are abundant in the Earth's crust, breeder reactors could supply us with power long after the more limited supplies of uranium are depleted. The Soviet Union already has a breeder reactor producing electrical power, and the United States has embarked upon a program to develop commercially viable breeder reactors by the mid-1980s.

In the following chapters we examine in greater detail the points raised in this introductory discussion. We consider how we use energy, our changing patterns of energy supply, and the consequences of using energy in various forms.

Chapter 2
WORK, ENERGY, AND POWER

We all have some intuitive notions about the quantity that is the central topic of this book—*energy*. We know that we must buy gasoline to supply the energy that runs our automobiles, and we pay a monthly bill to the electric company for the electrical energy that is delivered to our homes. We understand that coal, oil, and gas play important roles in supplying the energy that is necessary for our everyday living. But to pursue our topic in detail we need more than these qualitative ideas. We need to understand some of the basic physical principles that govern situations involving energy.

Before we can begin a meaningful discussion of energy problems, we must establish the language we will use. That is, we must define the terms and the units that are necessary to describe various situations involving energy. We will require only a few of the large number of the terms that apply to physical quantities—primarily, *work, energy,* and *power*. The units we will use are *metric* units—meters, kilograms, and seconds, as well as a few derived units such as watts and kilowatt-hours. Thus, we will employ only a limited vocabulary, one designed to cover only the situations of immediate interest.

THE DEFINITION OF WORK

We frequently use the term *work* in ordinary conversation. We might say, for example, "That job requires a great deal of work." What does "work" really mean here? If you lift a number of heavy boxes from floor level and place them on a high shelf, you will feel tired after the job is completed—you will know that you have done *work*. This is exactly right. Gravity pulls the boxes downward and when you lift the boxes, you are doing work against the gravitational force.

In its physical meaning, *work* always involves overcoming some opposing force. Suppose that instead of lifting one of the boxes, you push it across a rough floor. In this case, you are not working against the gravitational force—the box is at the same height throughout the movement. Instead, you are now working against the frictional force that exists between the moving box and the floor.

How do we measure work? The amount of work done in any situation depends on how much force was exerted and on how far the object moved. Increasing either the applied force or the distance through which the object is moved increases the amount of work done. That is, the work done is proportional to both the applied force and the distance through which the force acts (Fig. 2.1). The equation which expresses this statement is

$$\text{Work} = \text{force} \times \text{distance}$$

$$W = F \times d \qquad (2.1)$$

In this equation, d stands for the distance of movement, measured in meters (m), and F stands for the applied force. According to Newton's law of dynamics, $F = Ma$, the force F necessary to impart an acceleration a of 1 meter per second per second (1 m/s^2) to a mass M of 1 kilogram (1 kg), is 1 kg-m/s^2. To this unit we give the special name, 1 newton (1 N). Therefore, in Eq. 2.1, we have

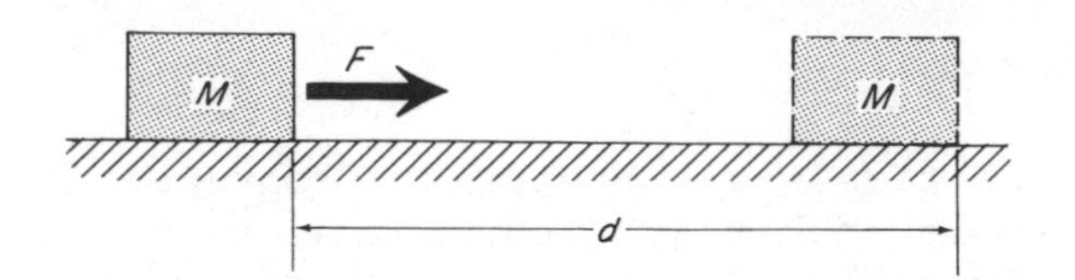

Figure 2.1 The work done by the force F is $W = Fd$.

F = force (in newtons)

d = distance (in meters)

W = work done (in newton-meters)

We give to the unit of work the special name *joule*:

$$1 \text{ joule (J)} = 1 \text{ newton-meter (N-m)} \tag{2.2}$$

How much work must be done to lift a block of mass M through a vertical height h? In this case, work is done against the gravitational force. The magnitude of this force is the *weight* of the object and is given by Newton's equation $F = Ma$, when we identify a as the acceleration due to gravity. We usually indicate the gravitational acceleration by the symbol g, so that the expression for the weight of an object (the gravitational force acting on the object) is

$$\text{Weight,} \quad w = F_{grav} = Mg \tag{2.3}$$

The value of g on or near the surface of the Earth is 9.8 m/s^2.

Now, we can use Eq. 2.1 to write the work required to lift a block of mass M through a vertical height h:

$$W = F_{grav} \times d = w \times h = Mgh$$

That is,

$$\boxed{\text{Work done in raising an object,} \quad W = Mgh} \tag{2.4}$$

If the mass is $M = 10$ kg and the height is $h = 3$ m, the work done is

$$W = Mgh$$

$$= (10 \text{ kg}) \times (9.8 \text{ m/s }) \times (3 \text{ m})$$

$$= 294 \text{ J}$$

A mass of 1 kg corresponds to 2.2 pounds (lb) and 1 m is a bit more than 3 feet (ft). Therefore, the amount of work done in this example corresponds approximately to that required to lift a 22-lb mass to the height of a basketball basket (10 ft).

ENERGY

When an object is moved against a force, work is done and *energy* is expended in the process by the agency responsible for the movement. Thus, we say, "A person must have a lot of energy to do a hard day's work." In fact, one way to define energy is

Energy is the capacity to do work.

Suppose that a cart is rolling at constant velocity v across a floor and strikes a block at rest on the floor (Fig. 2.2). As a result of the collision, the block will

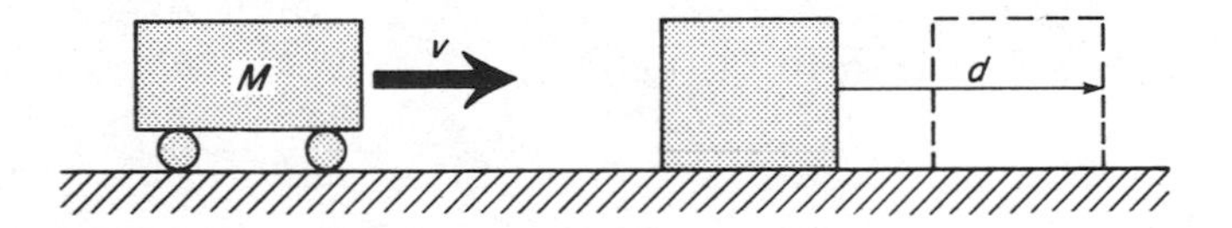

Figure 2.2 The kinetic energy of the moving cart is transferred to the block in a collision and the block slides across the floor. The sliding block does work against the frictional force.

slide a certain distance d across the floor before coming to rest because of friction. The sliding block has moved against the frictional force and has therefore done a certain amount of work.

The block moved and did work because energy was supplied to it by the moving cart. The energy that an object possesses *by virtue of its motion* is called *kinetic energy*. The more massive the object is and the faster it moves, the greater is its kinetic energy. The expression for the kinetic energy of an object with a mass M moving with a velocity v is

$$\text{Kinetic energy,} \quad \text{KE} = \frac{1}{2} Mv^2 \qquad (2.5)$$

Notice that the kinetic energy depends on the *square* of the velocity. A block moving with a velocity of 16 m/s has a kinetic energy *4* times greater than when it is moving with a velocity of 8 m/s.

What is the kinetic energy of a 12-kg object when it moves with a velocity of 7 m/s? Using Eq. 2.5,

$$\text{KE} = \frac{1}{2} Mv^2 = \frac{1}{2} \times (12 \text{ kg}) \times (7 \text{ m/s})^2 = 294 \text{ J}$$

which turns out to be exactly enough energy to raise a 10-kg object to a height of 3 m, as we found in the preceding section.

Notice that kinetic energy and work have the same units, namely, *joules*. We can see this more clearly by writing the units for the various physical quantities in the expressions for work and kinetic energy:

$$\begin{aligned} \text{Work} &= F \times d \\ &= (\text{N}) \times (\text{m}) \\ &= (\text{kg-m/s}^2) \times (\text{m}) \end{aligned}$$

$= (\text{kg-m}^2/\text{s}^2)$

$= (\text{J})$

$$\text{KE} = \frac{1}{2} Mv^2$$

$= (\text{kg}) \times (\text{m/s})^2$

$= (\text{kg-m}^2/\text{s}^2)$

$= (\text{J})$

In the preceding section we considered lifting a mass M to a height h. We found that the work done in such a case is $W = Mgh$. The object was originally at rest and in its final position the velocity is again zero. Thus, no kinetic energy was imparted to the object. But the object has a capability to do work that it did not have in its original position. For example, if we drop the object and allow it to fall through the height h, work can be done in driving a stake into the ground (Fig. 2.3). That is, the raised block has the *potential* to do work and we call this capability the *potential energy* of the object:

$$\boxed{\text{Potential energy, PE} = Mgh} \quad (2.6)$$

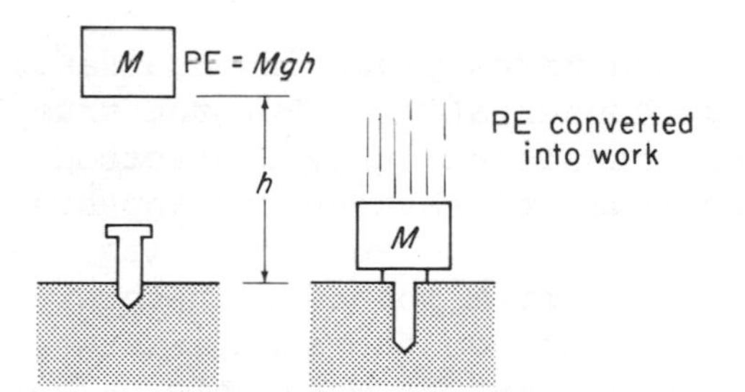

Figure 2.3 The potential energy of a raised block can be converted into work.

In falling toward the stake, the block *loses* potential energy (because h decreases), but it *gains* kinetic energy (because v increases). During the fall, the energy of the block is partly potential energy and partly kinetic energy. Just before striking the stake, *all* of the potential energy, Mgh, has been converted into kinetic energy so that $1/2\ Mv^2 = Mgh$. The potential energy is first converted into kinetic energy and then the kinetic energy is converted into work in driving the stake into the ground.

An appreciation for the amount of energy that is involved in various physical processes can be obtained by referring to Table 2.1. Notice that we use here (and throughout the remainder of this book) the *exponential* or *powers-of-ten* notation. The reader unfamiliar with this method of expressing large and small numbers should refer to Appendix I.

CONSERVATION OF ENERGY—FORMS OF ENERGY

In the example of the falling block driving the stake into the ground, no energy was lost in any phase of the process. An amount of work Mgh was required to lift the block from ground level to the height h and in this position the block possessed a potential energy Mgh. As the block fell, the sum of its potential and kinetic energies was always Mgh. Finally, the block did an amount of work Mgh on the stake. Energy was converted from one form to another, but no energy was lost. The same is true in *any* type of process—*energy is conserved.*

Every process known in Nature takes place in accordance with the principle of energy conservation. But the true importance of this principle cannot be fully understood or appreciated unless it is realized that energy appears in many forms. If we add up all of the energy in its various forms that an isolated system possesses before an event or process takes place and do the same afterward, we always find an exact balance. We can make this calculation only if we know all of the ways in which energy can appear. If we did not realize the existence of potential energy, for example, we would discover many situations

TABLE 2.1
Range of Energies in Physical Processes (Joules)

10^{42}	
	Supernova explosion
10^{38}	
10^{34}	Sun's output in 1 year
10^{30}	Rotational energy of Earth
10^{26}	Earth's annual energy from Sun
10^{22}	
	Severe earthquake
10^{18}	H-bomb
10^{14}	First atomic bomb
	Rocket launch
10^{10}	Lightning bolt
	8 hr of hard labor
10^{6}	
	Lethal dose of X radiation
10^{2}	Rifle bullet
10^{-2}	Half-dollar falling 3 ft
10^{-6}	Beat of fly's wing
10^{-10}	
	Fission of a uranium nucleus
10^{-14}	
	Electron in hydrogen atom
10^{-18}	Chemical bond

in which there is an apparent increase or decrease in energy.

We have discussed only two forms of energy thus far: the energy due to motion—*kinetic energy*—and the energy due to the gravitational attraction of the Earth for an object—*gravitational potential energy*. Both kinetic and potential energy can manifest themselves in other ways.

The molecules in every piece of matter—solid, liquid, or gas—are in a continual state of motion. This random, agitated motion constitutes an *internal* kinetic energy or *thermal energy* that an object possesses even though the object as a whole may not be in motion. A change in the internal energy of an object can be brought about by supplying *heat* to the object or by doing *work* on the object. If we do work on an object (for example, by repeatedly hitting a block of metal with a hammer), the molecules are caused to move more rapidly; the internal energy is thereby raised and there is an accompanying increase in *temperature*. Heat considerations are particularly important in processes that involve friction because the energy that is expended in working against frictional forces always appears in the form of heat. Thus, in any real physical process some energy will be "lost" in the heating of the objects involved and their surroundings.

The transmission of *sound* from one point to another takes place when the sound source (for example, a vibrating speaker diaphragm) sets into motion the air molecules in its immediate vicinity. These molecules collide with other nearby molecules and further molecular collisions cause the propagation of the sound to other points. Thus, sound is due to molecular motions and constitutes another form of kinetic energy.

If we raise an object near the surface of the Earth to a higher position, the work done in accomplishing this relocation is the *gravitational potential energy* of the object. In this case work is done against the attractive gravitational force. Work can also be done against electrical forces, and the potential energy that results is called the *electrical potential energy*.

When gasoline burns or when dynamite explodes, the potential energy stored in the substance is converted into heat or motional energy. When the fuel *methane*, CH_4 (the primary component of *natural gas*), burns to completion, the oxidation reaction is

$$CH_4 + 2\ O_2 \longrightarrow CO_2 + 2\ H_2O$$

The burning of 1 g of methane releases approximately 55,000 J of energy (which can be used to heat some other material). Where does this energy come from? We can represent the oxidation reaction in the following schematic way:

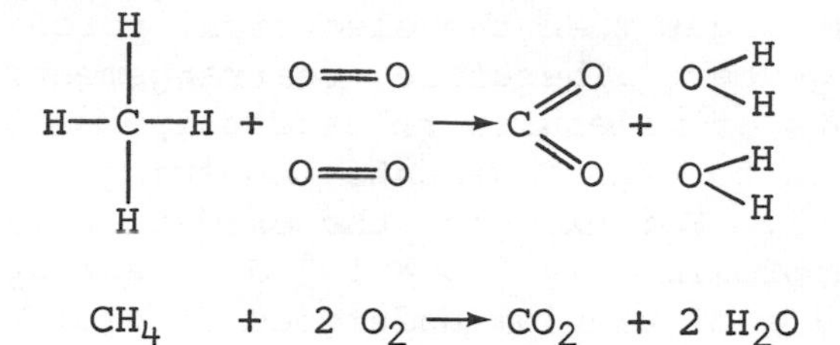

$$CH_4 + 2\ O_2 \rightarrow CO_2 + 2\ H_2O$$

where each short line connecting two element symbols represents a pair of electrons that bind the two atoms together. In order for the reaction to proceed, several atomic bonds must be broken and new ones formed:

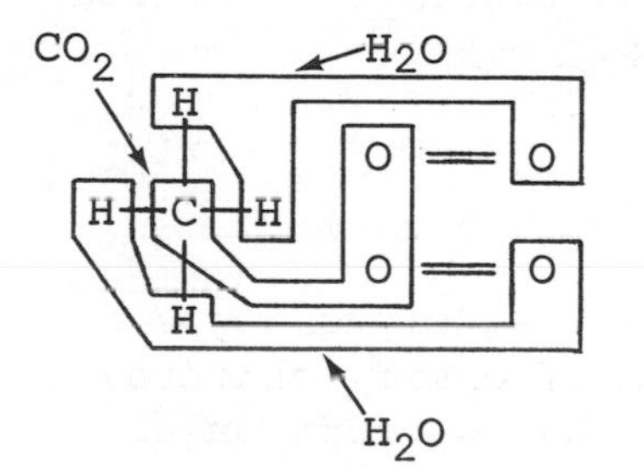

There is a certain amount of electrical potential energy in every molecule which is due to the arrangement of electrons around the positively charged nuclei. Some arrangements of electrons and nuclei have more potential energy than others. There is *more* electrical potential energy in the combination $CH_4 + 2\ O_2$ than when the same atoms are in the arrangement $CO_2 + 2\ H_2O$. Thus, the oxidation of methane to produce carbon dioxide and water *releases* energy. All forms of *chemical energy* are basically *electrical* in character.

The rearrangement of atoms to form different molecules involves energy changes. The chemical processes that take place when fuels are burned *release* energy. Similarly, the rearrangement of neutrons and protons to form different nuclei also involves energy changes. Some changes of this type require the *input* of energy, whereas others *release* energy. For example, when a uranium nucleus undergoes fission and splits into two nuclei of smaller mass, energy is released. The force that holds nuclei together—the *nuclear force*—is much stronger than the electrical force which holds molecules together. Therefore, rearrangements involving the constituents of molecules release only small amounts of energy compared to rearrangements involving the constituents of nuclei. For example, the oxidation of 1 g of CH_4 releases approximately 5.5×10^4 J of energy. But if every nucleus in 1 g of uranium undergoes fission, the energy released will be approximately 8×10^{10} J—more than a million times greater!

The fact that small amounts of matter can release enormous amounts of energy in the fission process is the basis for our nuclear energy industry. We return to the discussion of nuclear energy in Chapter 5.

ENERGY CONVERSION

Energy occurs in many forms and is readily changed from one form into another. We make use of energy conversion processes every day. For example, when we turn on an electric switch, electrical energy is converted into radiant energy (light) and thermal energy (heat) by an electric lamp. Our bodies convert the chemical energy in foodstuffs into mechanical energy whenever we move a muscle. And we use the chemical energy in storage batteries to operate the electrical starters in our automobile engines.

The conversion of energy from one form to another plays an extremely important role in the energy distribution network. If we require energy to operate an electrical motor, the ultimate source of that energy is the radiant energy from the Sun, which in turn results from nuclear reactions taking place deep in the Sun's interior. Figure 2.4 shows in a schematic way the various steps in this process. Several different energy conversions are involved:

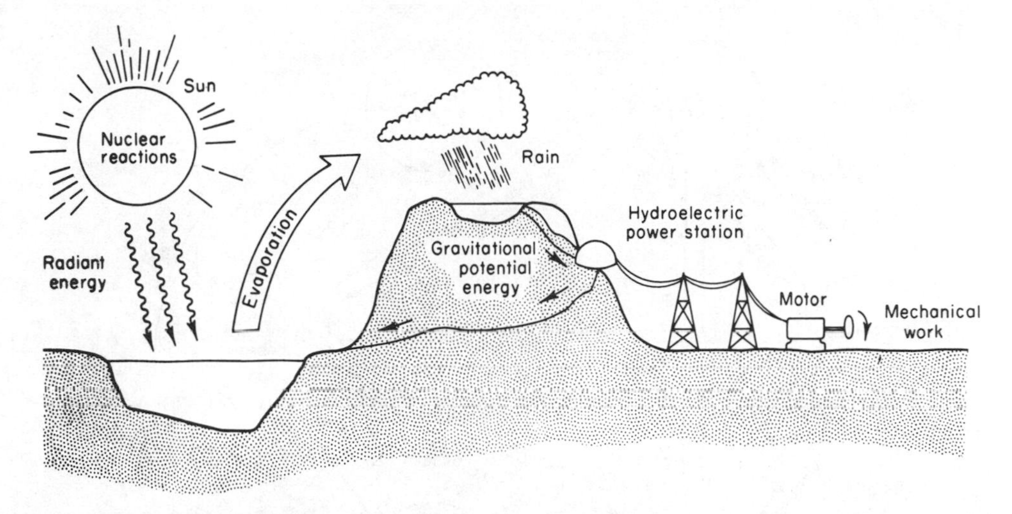

Figure 2.4 Energy changes form many times between the release of nuclear energy in the Sun and the ultimate utilization of that energy in doing mechanical work.

nuclear energy → radiant energy → thermal energy → gravitational potential energy → electrical energy → mechanical work. If we stored the electrical energy as chemical energy in a battery before using it to drive the motor, we could add still another step in the sequence.

Potential energy is always due to the presence of a *force*, and there are only *three* basic types of forces in Nature—gravitational, electrical, and nuclear. (Actually, there are *two* distinct types of nuclear forces, but this need not concern us here.) Therefore, we should really classify all energy into only four categories—motional or kinetic energy and three types of potential energy. However, it proves convenient to deviate from this strict scheme and to use such labels as chemical energy, radiant energy, and thermal energy. Various kinds of devices or processes can be used to convert energy from one of these forms into another.

Figure 2.5 shows some of the primary connections among the different energy forms. Notice that some of these energy changes are reversible: for example, radiant

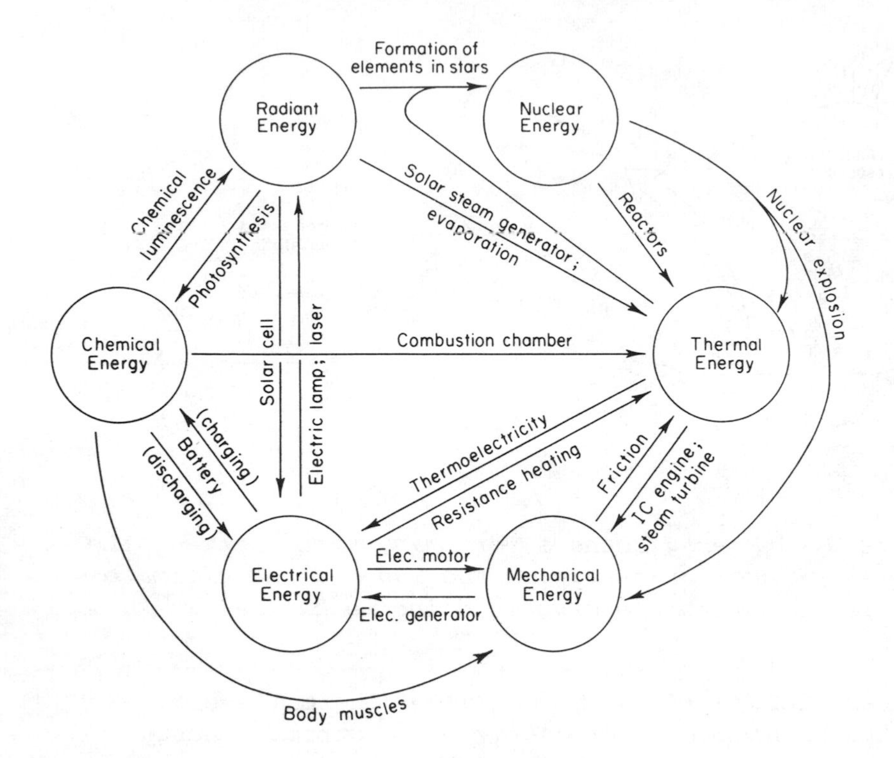

Figure 2.5 Important forms of energy and some of the principal conversion pathways that connect them.

energy can be converted into electrical energy (with a solar cell) and electrical energy can be converted into radiant energy (with an electric lamp). On the other hand, some changes are essentially "one-way streets." It is easy to convert chemical energy into thermal energy (by combustion), but the reverse process (taken directly) is difficult to achieve. If we wish to convert thermal energy into chemical energy by conventional methods, we could use the thermal energy to drive a steam turbine which would operate an electrical generator which would charge a battery.

EFFICIENCY IN ENERGY CONVERSIONS

A *machine* is any device that can extract energy from some source and convert this energy into useful work. The energy source might be the potential energy in water stored behind a dam, the chemical (electrical) energy in gasoline or coal, or the radiant energy in sunlight. Various machines have been constructed to utilize the energy from these and other sources. No machine, however, can completely convert available energy into useful work. By one means or another, energy always manages to escape to the surroundings in any conversion process. Friction exists in every moving system and the effect of friction is to convert energy from the source into thermal energy, thereby raising the temperature of the surroundings. An operating automobile engine becomes hot and the thermal energy in the engine block cannot be recovered and used to assist in propelling the vehicle. In other situations, such as the explosion of a stick of dynamite, some of the energy is released in the form of light and sound.

Every machine can be characterized by an *efficiency*, which is the ratio of the useful work performed to the amount of energy used in the process:

$$\text{Efficiency} = e = \frac{\text{work done}}{\text{energy used}} \tag{2.7}$$

Schematically, the situation is that pictured in Fig. 2.6. An energy source (for example, a tank of gasoline) delivers an amount of energy E to an engine. A fraction eE (where e is some number between 0 and 1) appears as useful work—for example, in the motional energy of the automobile.

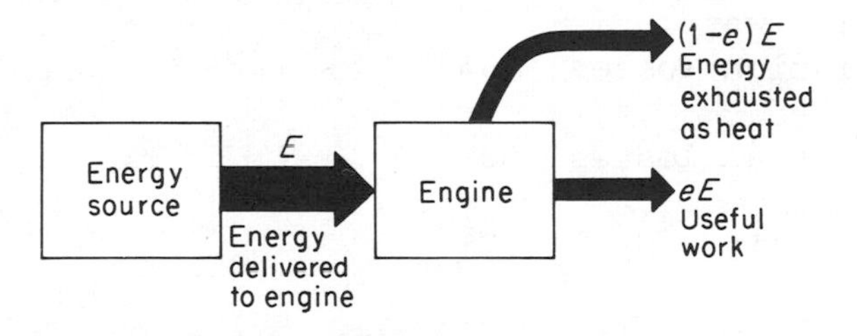

Figure 2.6 The flow of energy through an engine whose operating efficiency is e.

The remainder, $(1 - e)E$, appears in the form of heat. Almost all machines that are used on a wide and regular basis have efficiencies less than 0.5 (50 percent). An automobile engine typically has an efficiency of about 25 percent (the figure varies depending on how well the engine is tuned and on the operating speed). The best steam engine has an efficiency of only about 10 percent. In a coal-fired electricity-generating plant, a maximum of about 40 percent of the chemical energy in the fuel can be converted into electrical energy. Further losses occur in the transmission of this energy and in its utilization in the consumer's device. If the energy is used in an electrical heating system, essentially all of the electrical energy is converted into thermal energy. On the other hand, if it is used to drive an electric motor (efficiency about 25 percent), the *overall* efficiency will be only about 10 percent.

It is important to realize that energy is not "lost" in any of these processes, no matter how inefficient. The energy lost by one part of a system always appears in some other part of the system or in some other form, such as heat. Energy is always conserved.

The examination of a particular case will serve to emphasize the problem of efficiency in energy conversions. Consider the case of a typical coal-burning electrical generating plant. What happens to the original available chemical energy? The tabulation below shows the various losses that occur in the generating process:

Original chemical energy in coal		100%
Heat lost in stack gases	10%	
Heat lost in cooling water	50%	
Electrical transmission losses	3%	
Total losses	63%	
Electrical energy delivered	37%	

This overall efficiency of 37 percent represents about the best that can now be done in the generation of electricity from chemical fuels. However, it must be mentioned that the efficiency of a machine or of an electrical generating plant depends to some extent on the physical and economic constraints that are placed on the system. Consider the design of a coal-fired generating plant. The construction of the facility will cost a certain amount of money (including interest charges on borrowed capital), and the operation (including fuel charges) will cost a certain amount annually. The object is to produce electricity which can be sold at competitive prices, and still allow for all operating costs to be met as well as for the amortization of the capital expenditures over some period of time (typically 30 years). With no other constraints, there is a certain optimum design which results in a certain operating efficiency. Depending on fuel and construction costs (and interest rates), the efficiency might be rather low—perhaps 30 percent. To improve the efficiency, and thereby reduce the amount of fuel consumed, might result in an unacceptable increase in construction costs. A number of factors could be introduced to alter the economics of the design. For example, if the price of coal were doubled or tripled, or if interest rates were reduced, it would become practical to expend more money on construction to improve efficiency and reduce the fuel costs. Or, the constraint could be of a different type. Every generating plant produces waste heat. Usually, this heat is exhausted into bodies of water (a river or a bay), with the consequent raising of the local water temperature. The *thermal pollution* so produced will have effects on the marine life. If it is judged that these effects are seriously detrimental to the ecology of the water system, the amount of water heating produced by the generating plant would have to be reduced. Such a reduction calls for a change of design which, in turn, affects the efficiency and finally the price that must be charged for the electricity produced.

The rate at which we consume our fuel supplies depends on the efficiencies of the devices we use, and these efficiencies depend on a large number of factors. Within certain bounds, efficiency is a question of how much money we are willing to spend and of how many artificial constraints we wish to impose.

POWER

Two men do equal amounts of work by lifting identical boxes from floor level and placing them on a shelf. One of the men works rapidly and the other works slowly. Although the total amount of work performed by each man is the same, the two men have quite different bodily sensations when their tasks are completed. The reason is that the two men have been working at different *power* levels: The faster-working man was converting body chemical energy into work at a more rapid rate than was the slower-working man. It is difficult for the body to maintain a high rate of energy conversion and so the faster-working man feels a greater "drain" on his internal energy supply.

Power is the *rate* at which work is done or energy is used:

$$\text{Power} = \frac{\text{work done (or energy used)}}{\text{time}}$$

$$P = \frac{W}{t} \qquad (2.8)$$

Work is measured in *joules* and time is measured in *seconds*, and so the unit of power is the *joule/second* (J/s). To this unit we give the special name, *watt* (W):

$$1 \text{ J/s} = 1 \text{ W} \qquad (2.9)$$

For large amounts of power, we use the following designations:

10^3 W = 1 kilowatt = 1 kW

10^6 W = 1 megawatt = 1 MW

Another unit of power that is often used is the *horsepower* (hp). This unit is now defined in terms of the watt:

$$1 \text{ hp} = 746 \text{ W} \simeq \frac{3}{4} \text{ kW} \qquad (2.10)$$

A term that we frequently hear about or see on our electric bills is the *kilowatt-hour*. The kilowatt is a unit of power and the hour is a unit of time. Therefore, the kilowatt-hour is a unit of (power) × (time). According to Eq. 2.8, (power) × (time) = (energy). Thus, the kilowatt-hour (kWh) is a unit of energy. We can express 1 kWh in joules:

$$1 \text{ kWh} = P \times t = (1000 \text{ W}) \times (1 \text{ hr}) \times \frac{3600 \text{ s}}{1 \text{ hr}}$$

$$= 3.6 \times 10^6 \text{ W-s} = 3.6 \times 10^6 \text{ J}$$

It is important to understand the distinction between *power* and *energy* (or *work*), and it is important to understand that *kilowatts* and *kilowatt-hours* refer to two different physical quantities. *Power is the rate at which work is done or the rate at which energy is used.*

Some appreciation for the power levels that we find in everyday devices can be gained by referring to Table 2.2. Notice that the continuous power output of an active human body is limited to a few hundred watts. However, for brief intervals, the power figure can be substantially higher. For example, for the fraction of a second that a high-jumper requires to launch himself off the ground, his body is operating with a power of about 3 kW.

Electrical generating plants are huge complexes that devour enormous quantities of fuel in the production of electrical power. Many of the large modern plants produce more than 1000 MW (10^9 W) of power. In discussing the power ratings of these plants, we must be careful to distinguish between the *thermal* or *input* power and the *electrical* or *output* power. Usually we indicate this by placing a t after the MW rating to denote thermal power and by using an e to denote electrical power. Thus, a

TABLE 2.2
Operating Power Levels of Various Devices (Watts)

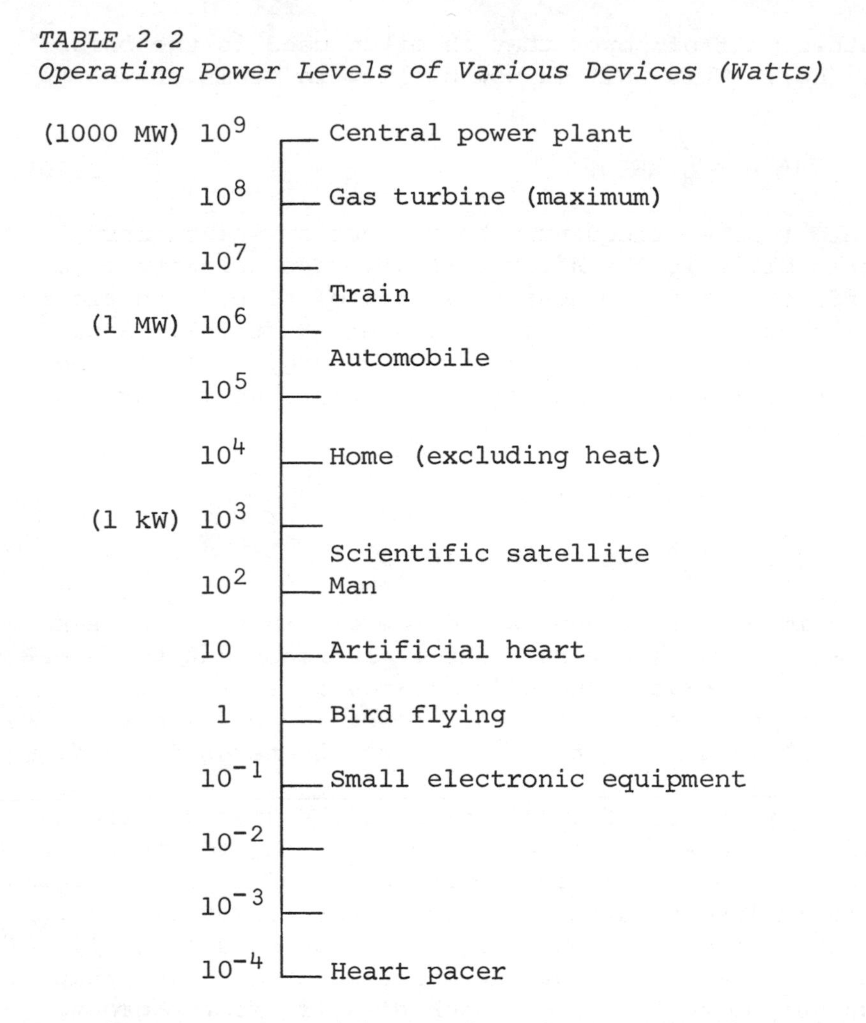

particular plant might produce 3000 MW of thermal power (3000 MWt) but, because of the losses in converting thermal energy into electrical energy, the output power might be only 1000 MW of electrical power (1000 MWe).

ENERGY UNITS AND CONVERSIONS

The basic unit for the measurement of energy in the metric system is the *joule*. But we also find other units in common usage. The *kilowatt-hour* is often used in discussions of electrical energy, and this is the main unit used in the remainder of this book. The *Calorie* is also used, primarily in heat problems and to describe the energy content of foodstuffs. The *British thermal unit* (BTU) is not a metric unit, but it is frequently used (particularly by engineers) in energy calculations. The conversion factors that relate these units are given in Table 2.3.

TABLE 2.3
Energy Conversion Factors

	Value in joules	Value in kilowatt-hours	Value in BTU
1 joule	1	2.78×10^{-7}	0.95×10^{-3}
1 kilowatt-hour	3.6×10^{6}	1	3.41×10^{3}
1 Calorie	4186	1.16×10^{-3}	3.97
1 BTU	1055	2.93×10^{-4}	1

In the following chapters we will be discussing the various fuels that are in use today. It will be convenient to have a list showing the energy that can be derived from these sources. Some of this information is summarized in Table 2.4. In each case the energy is given in metric units for the common unit of measure for the fuel. The values are also given in British thermal units to facilitate comparisons with other references where these units are used. Notice that the energy released in the fission of 1 g of uranium is several times greater than that released in burning 1 ton of coal.

Table 2.5 shows the amounts of various fuels required by an electrical generating plant to produce 1000 MWe of output electrical power. By way of comparison, it should be noted that a high quality oil well can produce from 3,000 to 10,000 barrels of crude oil per day, and a high quality gas well can produce from 5 to 20 million cubic feet of natural gas per day.

TABLE 2.4
Energy Content of Various Fuels

Fuel	Amount	Energy		
		Joules	Kilowatt-hours	BTU
Coal	1 ton (2000 lb)	2.8×10^{10}	7800	2.7×10^{7}
Oil	1 barrel (42 gal)	6.1×10^{9}	1700	5.8×10^{6}
Natural gas	1 cubic foot (ft^3)	1.0×10^{6}	0.29	0.95×10^{3}
Wood	1 ton	1.0×10^{10}	2900	0.95×10^{7}
TNT (explosion)	1 ton	4.4×10^{9}	1200	4.2×10^{6}
Gasoline	1 gallon	1.3×10^{8}	36	1.2×10^{5}
Uranium (fission)	1 gram	8.2×10^{10}	2.3×10^{4}	7.8×10^{7}
Deuterium (fusion)	1 gram	2.4×10^{11}	6.6×10^{4}	2.3×10^{8}

TABLE 2.5
Fuel Requirements of a 1000-MWe (3000-MWt) Power Plant

Fuel	Amount required for 1000 MWe
Coal	9000 tons/day (1 trainload/day)
Oil	40,000 barrels/day (1 tanker/week)
Natural gas	2.5×10^{6} ft^3/day
Uranium	3 kg/day

QUESTIONS AND EXERCISES

1. An amount of work equal to 2 J is required to compress the spring in a spring-gun. To what height can the spring-gun fire a 10-g projectile? What is the velocity of the projectile as it leaves the spring-gun?

2. The pumping action of the heart gives to the blood some kinetic energy. Where does this energy originate and what happens to the blood's kinetic energy?

3. What is the power of an engine that lifts a 1000-kg mass to a height of 100 m in 3 min?

4. Classify the energy in the following systems according to *basic* energy forms: (a) water in a storage tower, (b) sonic boom, (c) food, (d) boiling water, and (e) moving automobile.

5. Some devices are said to "waste" energy. Is such a statement strictly true? What happens to the "wasted" energy?

6. A certain power plant operates at an efficiency of 40 percent and produces an output electrical power of 500 MWe. How much coal (in tons per hour) does the plant burn?

7. A gallon of oil has a mass of 7.5 lb. What is the energy content of 1 ton of oil? Compare with the value for coal. (Use Table 2.4.)

8. An automobile makes a 50-mile trip in 1 hr and uses 5 gal of gasoline in the process. At what average horsepower did the automobile operate during the trip? The figure you calculate will be somewhat larger than the horsepower rating of most standard-sized automobiles. Why?

Chapter 3
ENERGY CONSUMPTION—TODAY AND THE FUTURE

Present-day society consumes energy at a fantastic pace. Almost every aspect of modern civilization is geared to the use of energy. The magnitude of the industrialized world's usage of energy can be appreciated by noting that *half* of the energy that has ever been used by Man has been used during the last 100 years. As a result, the business of providing energy has become one of our primary occupations. Billions upon billions of dollars have been expended in the construction of hydroelectric dams, petroleum refining plants, and power generating stations, as well as in the ever wider search for fuel deposits in the Earth. About 10 percent of the gross national product (GNP) of the United States is derived from the business of producing energy—this amounts to about $100 billion per year!

In this chapter we examine the ways in which energy is used in our modern world, and in the next chapter we discuss the various sources of our energy.

HOW MUCH ENERGY DO WE USE?

When we discuss the energy used by the entire world population or even that used in the United States alone, the figures are so tremendous that we tend to lose sight of their significance. Therefore, let us begin by looking at the energy balance sheet for a typical U.S. citizen. The average intake of food energy by an individual in the United States (one of the best-fed countries in the world) amounts to about 3000 Calories per day. In the course of a day's activities, the individual expends an equal amount of energy in doing work and in maintaining the life functions of his body. According to the conversion factor listed in Table 2.3, 3000 Cal is equivalent to 3.5 kWh. At this same rate of energy consumption, the individual requires about 3000 kWh of food energy each year. (Do not be confused by the use of the kilowatt-hour to measure food energy. Although we tend to think of the kilowatt-hour as an electrical unit, it is actually an *energy* unit and can be used to measure any form of energy.)

In addition to food energy, a person uses energy in many other forms: electrical energy for home and office lighting, chemical energy to operate his automobile, the energy represented in the products he buys, and so forth. In fact, food energy accounts for only a small fraction of the total energy used by any individual in a civilized country today. The average amount of energy used by a person in the United States per year is approximately 100,000 (10^5) kWh, about 75 times more than the food energy alone!

If we multiply 10^5 kWh by the U.S. population (200,000,000 $= 2 \times 10^8$), we arrive at a figure of 2×10^{13} kWh for the annual consumption of energy in all forms in the United States—this is 20,000 *billion* kilowatt-hours!

The United States is the world's major user of energy. This country accounts for about one-third of the worldwide consumption of energy. That is,

Current U.S. energy consumption $\simeq 2 \times 10^{13}$ kWh/y

Current worldwide energy consumption $\simeq 6 \times 10^{13}$ kWh/y

In order to appreciate these staggering figures, it is useful to note that the amount of energy consumed per year in the United States is equivalent to that obtained by burning approximately 3.5 billion (3.5×10^9) tons of coal.

Not only does the United States consume more energy than any other country, we also use more energy per capita than any other nation in the world. The United States has only 6 percent of the world's population, and yet we account for one-third of the world's energy consumption. That is, the per capita use of energy in the United States is more than 5 times the worldwide average. A person in the United States consumes, on the average, about twice as much energy as a person in the highly developed countries of Western Europe. But compared to the poor nations of Asia, the per capita use of energy in this country is greater by a factor of about 30. In fact, the GNP per capita for a country (a good measure of its wealth and standard of living) goes hand in hand with its per capita energy consumption. Energy breeds wealth, and wealth is utilized in buying goods and services that require energy. And the more energy that a wealthy nation has at its disposal, the less efficiently it tends to be utilized.

HOW DO WE USE OUR ENERGY?

In what ways do we use energy? We can identify four major categories of energy usage: residential, commercial, industrial, and transportation. Figure 3.1 shows the percentages of the total U.S. energy consumption attributable to these sectors of our economy. Any particular item that uses energy might contribute to more than one sector. For example, consider a home appliance. The electrical energy used by the appliance appears in the residential category. But energy was required in the manufacture of the appliance (industrial), in moving it to the merchant's store (transportation), and in the overhead expenditures of the merchant's operation (commercial).

Let us look more closely at energy usage in the residential sector. Table 3.1 shows the primary ways in which we use energy in our homes. Notice that home air-conditioning uses about 140 billion kWh per year or about 0.7

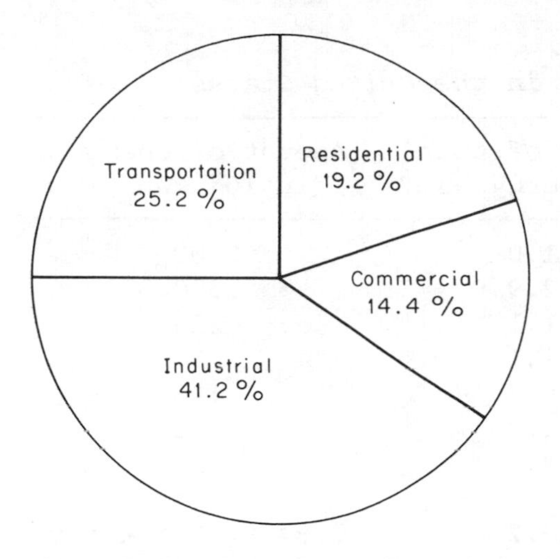

Figure 3.1 Energy usage in the four major sectors of the U.S. economy.

percent of the total burden of our energy resources in 1973. Although this figure is small in terms of the *total* energy usage, residential and commercial air-conditioning is the most rapidly growing item in the energy usage list. Air-conditioners can represent a substantial load on the local electrical generating facilities during exceptionally hot weather. In fact, the extra demand for electrical power to operate air-conditioning equipment during "heat waves" often taxes the ability of utility companies to meet the demand. In such situations, the line voltage is sometimes reduced by up to 5 percent--and causes a "brownout."

It is not feasible to lower the line voltage by more than about 5 percent in brownout conditions because a further reduction would damage many types of electric motors and electrically operated machinery. The alternative in exceptional situations is simply to cut off all power—a deliberate "blackout." (If the switches are not pulled to produce a deliberate blackout, overloads may result which will cause the generating or control equipment to fail—a much more serious type of blackout.

TABLE 3.1
Uses of Residential Energy in the United States

	Percent of total U.S. energy used	Amount of energy (in 10^9 kWh/y)
Space heating	11.0	2200
Water heating	2.9	580
Cooking	1.1	220
Refrigeration	1.1	220
Air-conditioning	0.7	140
Clothes drying	0.3	60
Other	2.1	420
Total	19.2	3.84×10^{12} kWh/y

Remember the massive blackout in the Northeast United States in November 1965!) If a deliberate blackout proves necessary, it is usually accomplished (as has been done in Britain) by blacking out a relatively small area for a few hours and then transferring the blackout to another area—a "rolling blackout."

The entry labeled "Other" in Table 3.1 includes home lighting and all of the many small appliances usually found in the home. Table 3.2 shows the estimated annual consumption of electrical energy by various major and small appliances. The cost for electrical energy varies considerably, depending on the distance of the consumer from the power plant, the cost of fuel used by the plant, and the quantity of energy used. A large user near a hydroelectric plant will generally pay the lowest rate; most household consumers pay 2 to 3 cents per kilowatt-hour. The annual cost figures given in the last column of Table 3.2 are based on a rate of 2 cents per kilowatt-hour. Because of the recent large increases in fuel prices, electrical charges have also jumped. In many areas of the country the cost per kilowatt-hour of electrical energy is a third higher than it was in early 1973.

TABLE 3.2
The Cost of Using Appliances[a]

Appliance	Estimated average annual kWh used	Annual cost (based on 2¢ per kWh)[b]
Air-conditioner (window)	1389	$27.78
Electric blanket	147	2.54
Carving knife	8	0.16
Clock	17	0.34
Clothes dryer	993	19.86
Clothes washer (automatic)	103	2.05
Dishwasher	353	7.26
Hairdryer	14	0.23
Humidifier	163	3.26
Range	1175	23.50
Refrigerator-freezer (frostless, 14 ft)	1829	36.58
Shaver	18	0.36
Television (color)	502	10.04
Toaster	39	0.78
Toothbrush	5	0.10
Vacuum cleaner	46	0.92
Water heater (quick recovery)	4811	96.22

[a]From *Changing Times, The Kiplinger Magazine*, November 1972.
[b]The cost per kWh of electrical energy has risen by about one-third since this table was prepared.

ENERGY USAGE IN THE FUTURE

The history of the American appetite for energy is one of continual increase. Figure 3.2 shows that the total energy consumption per year has undergone a 20-fold increase in the last 100 years. During this same period,

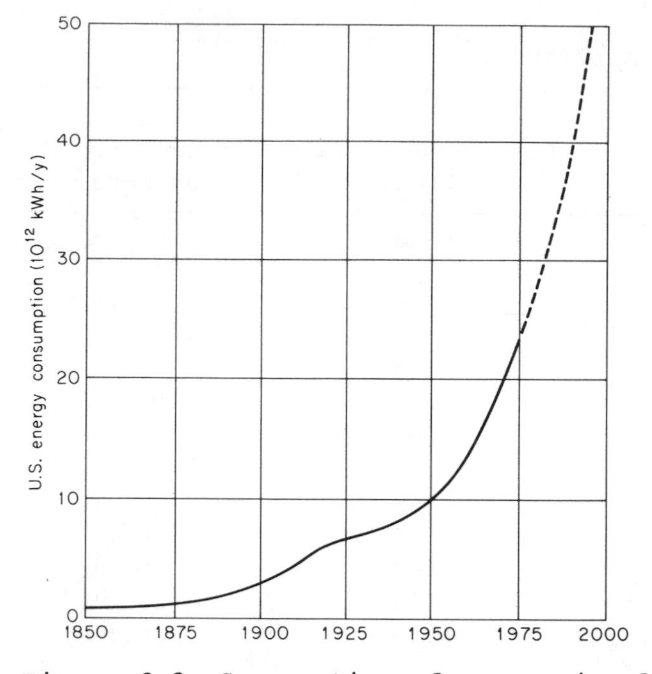

Figure 3.2 Consumption of energy in all forms per year in the United States since 1850.

the population has grown by a factor of 5. That is, we now use 4 times as much energy per person as we did in the 1870s.

The rate at which *electrical* energy is used in the United States is increasing at an even more rapid pace. In 1937, we used about 1000 kWh per person every year. In 1967, the annual figure stood at 6000 kWh per person, and in 1973 it was about 10,000 kWh per person.

How will our patterns of energy usage change in the future? First, it is quite certain that we will continue to use energy more rapidly in the future than we have in the past unless severe artificial constraints are placed on our consumption patterns. Projections for the remainder of this century indicate that in the United States we will have doubled our present rate of energy usage by about 1990. Figure 3.3 shows the estimates of energy

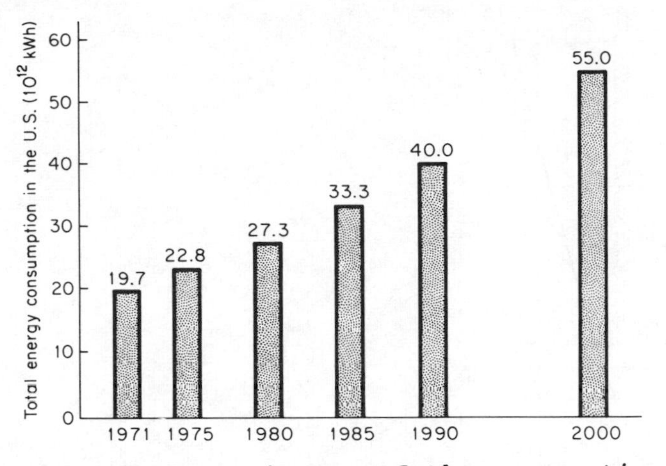

Figure 3.3 Estimates of the consumption of energy in the United States in the near future.

consumption extending into the future. In 1990 it is estimated that we will use about 40×10^{12} kWh of energy in the United States. It should be noted that these projections do not include the effects of conservation measures that could be instituted (including the reduction in demand by the levying of substantial fuel-use taxes). It is conceivable that a decrease in energy consumption of 15 percent from the projected figure could be realized by 1980, and even more by the year 2000.

Second, it is also clear that we are continuing to change toward an electrically oriented society. An increasing fraction of the energy that we use is in the form of electrical energy.* Figure 3.4 shows the tremendous growth rate of electrical energy usage in the United States from 1935 to the present.

In order to gauge the need for new electrical generating facilities, we must have an estimate of the demand for

---

*One of the problems associated with the growth of usage of electrical energy is that the transportation of electrical energy is by wires—*copper* wires—and we are beginning to experience a shortage of copper which may soon become severe.

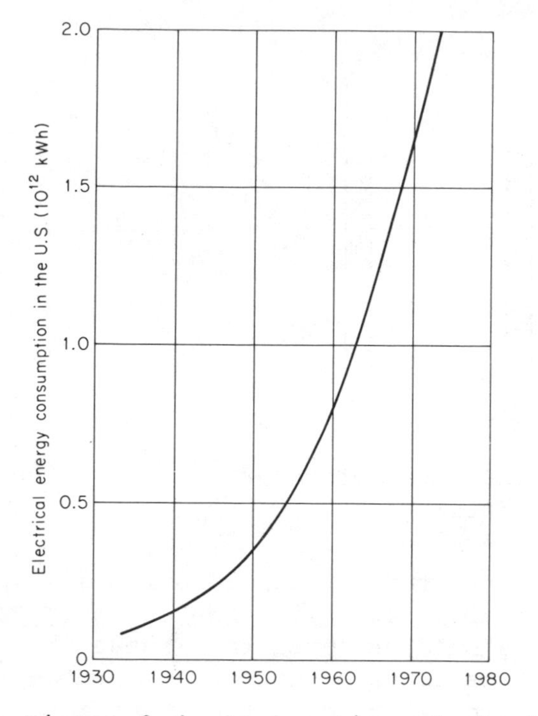

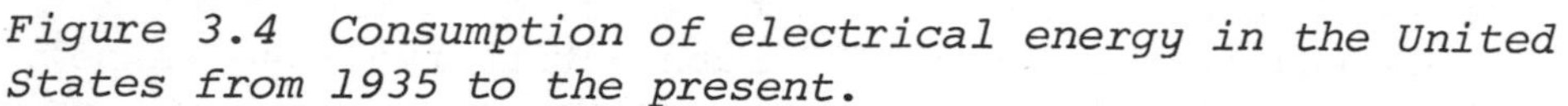
Figure 3.4 Consumption of electrical energy in the United States from 1935 to the present.

electrical energy in the future. But how can we use a steeply rising curve such as that in Fig. 3.4 to make this estimate? (Try extending the curve to the year 2000.) One way to make a forecast is to display the information on a graph that gives the vertical scale in factors of 10. A graph of this kind is called a *logarithmic* graph. Figure 3.5 shows that the curve in Fig. 3.4 becomes a straight line on a logarithmic graph. An extrapolation into the future is easy to make by simply extending the straight line. Of course, such a procedure assumes that the recent pattern of energy usage will continue into the future, but for the near term—10 to 20 years or so—the projections are probably not substantially in error.

By comparing Figs. 3.3 and 3.5, we can see that the electrical fraction of our total energy usage will approximately double between 1973 and 1990, increasing from about

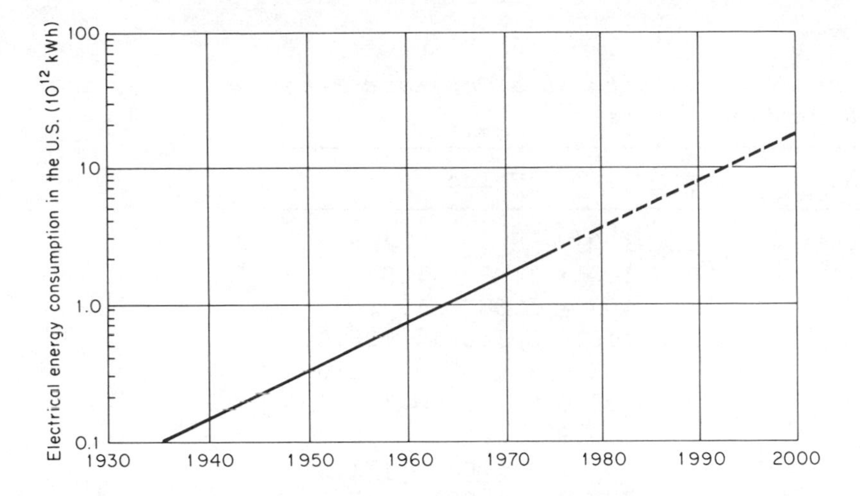

Figure 3.5 A logarithmic graph of the consumption of electrical energy in the United States. This information is the same as that shown in Fig. 3.4, but in this form, projections into the future are easier to make.

10 percent to about 20 percent. Looking even further into the future, it seems likely that about half of the energy we use will be in the form of electrical energy by early in the next century.

Another way to describe the rate of increase of a quantity is in terms of the percentage increase per year. For example, suppose that you invest $100 in a savings account and draw 8 percent compound interest (a very good rate!). At the end of 1 year, you would have $108. After 2 years, you would have 1.08 × $108 = $116.60, and after 3 years, you would have 1.08 × $116.60 = $126. Table 3.3 shows the annual increase in your account. After 9 years, you would have doubled your money to $200. This time—9 years in this case—is called the *doubling time* of the quantity. If we continued the calculation, we would find that, after 18 years, the account balance would have doubled again to $400.

The usage of electrical energy in the United States has been increasing in the recent past at a rate of about 8

TABLE 3.3
Increase of a Quantity at a Constant Rate of 8 Percent per Year

Year	Value
Base year	100
Year 1	100 × 1.08 = 108
2	108 × 1.08 = 116.6
3	116.6 × 1.08 = 126.0
4	126.0 × 1.08 = 136.0
5	136.0 × 1.08 = 146.9
6	146.9 × 1.08 = 158.7
7	158.7 × 1.08 = 171.4
8	171.4 × 1.08 = 185.1
9	185.1 × 1.08 = 200.0

percent per year. Therefore, we can look forward (at least in the near future) to the necessity of doubling our electrical generating capacity every 9 years.

Any quantity that increases at a constant percentage each year can be represented by a straight line on a logarithmic graph. (This type of increase is called an *exponential* increase.) If the annual percentage increase is not too great, we can obtain the doubling time from the following simple formula:

$$\text{Doubling time in years} = \frac{70}{\text{percentage increase per year}} \quad (3.1)$$

In our example above, we found a doubling time of 9 years for an annual percentage increase of 8 percent. Equation 3.1 gives 70/8 = 8.75 years, very close to the true value.

Not only is the use of electrical energy doubling every 9 years, but other energy-related activities show similar increasing trends. Table 3.4 lists the average annual percentage increases and doubling times for several different activities that influence our energy production and energy usage. The dramatic way in which increases

TABLE 3.4
Doubling Times of Energy-Related Activities

	Period	Annual percentage increase	Doubling time (years)
Electrical power	1955-1967	8.0	9.0
Passenger automobiles	1953-1966	6.7	10.4
Distance flown on passenger airlines	1953-1966	7.2	9.7
Tonnage of merchant shipping	1953-1967	4.9	14.2
Crude oil production	1890-1971	6.9	10.0
Coal production	1944-1971	3.6	19.8

have occurred in recent years emphasizes the increasing burden being placed upon our energy resources. According to the predictions shown in Fig. 3.3, the next doubling of our total energy usage will take place in about 20 years. This corresponds to a growth rate of 3.6 percent per year.

We can obtain an estimate of the future development of a particular quantity or activity by examining its performance during the past few years. In fact, this is essentially the only way in which we can gauge the near-term prospects in any area. Manufacturers regulate the output of their plants based on the expected demand for their products. The electrical power industry plans new generating facilities (which require many years for design and construction) on the basis of the expected requirements in the future.

Although it is clearly necessary to plan ahead, it is not prudent to place too much reliance on estimates that carry far into the future. The doubling time of 10.4 years for the number of passenger automobiles (see Table 3.4) is a result of the fact that the late 1950s and early 1960s were years of exceptional economic growth. If we use this doubling time to estimate the number of automobiles in this country in the year 2000, we come to the absurd conclusion that every person will own two or three automobiles. The extrapolation of a pattern of exponential increase into the future is valid only in the case of unconstrained growth. At some point, saturation sets in and lessens the rate of increase. The country would be saturated with automobiles long before the projection of two or three per person could be realized.

Long-term projections must be based on more than simple extrapolations of recent history. This is one of the problems that we face when attempting to forecast the demand for energy in the next century. Different experts will analyze the situation in different ways and will arrive at different predictions. For example, the U.S. Atomic Energy Commission (AEC) has estimated that 70 percent of our electrical power will be generated by nuclear power plants in the year 2000, but other projections place the figure nearer to 25 percent.

In making energy forecasts, the problem is doubly difficult. First, there is considerable uncertainty regarding the estimates of the available reserves of our various fuels. In addition, there are many difficult questions that must be asked: How will the changing birthrate in the United States and other countries influence the population picture? How rapidly will developing nations place increased demands on the energy supply? How readily will the population accept a trade-off of standard of living for environmental protection? How quickly can solar power or fusion power be made viable? In spite of the substantial difficulties, it is important to look ahead as best we can and to make the best effort to avoid the sudden confrontation with an unexpected problem. It is in this spirit that the estimates and projections discussed in this book have been made.

QUESTIONS AND EXERCISES

1. An average person requires about 3000 Cal of food energy each day. (1 Cal = 1.16×10^{-3} kWh.) Examine the lighting in a room of your home and estimate the amount of electrical energy used per day to operate the lights. Compare this electrical energy with your food energy requirements.

2. Is food an expensive source of energy? How much would your daily intake of food cost if it could be purchased according to energy content at the prevailing rate for electrical energy (2 cents/kWh)?

3. Suppose that all of the electrical energy used in the United States were purchased at the normal household rate of 2 cents/kWh (actually, industrial users pay less). Calculate your share of the bill by dividing the total annual cost by the U.S. population.

4. Use a figure of 2×10^{12} kWh for the consumption of electrical energy in the United States in 1973 and estimate the consumption in the years 1980 and 1990. (Use Table 3.3.) Do your figures agree with the extrapolated line in Fig. 3.5?

5. In 1971 the world production of crude oil amounted to 17.6 billion barrels (42 gal each). Estimate the production for the year 1977, based on the annual percentage increase figure given in Table 3.4.

6. The estimate of the world population in 1970 was 3.6 billion (3.6×10^9) and was increasing at an annual rate of 2 percent. The total land area of the world is 1.36×10^8 km^2. What was the 1970 population density in persons per square kilometer? If the rate of increase remains constant, what is the doubling time of the world population? Estimate the world population in the year 2500. How many square meters of the Earth's surface will be available for each person at that time? Do you believe that it is reasonable to estimate the world population this far

in the future by assuming a constant percentage increase? What factors have not been considered in making such an assumption?

Chapter 4
SOURCES OF ENERGY

During most of Man's history, wood was his only fuel. In the twelfth century A.D., coal was discovered on the northeast coast of England, near Newcastle, but the widespread adoption of this substance as a fuel did not take place for several hundred years. In fact, because the burning of the soft Newcastle coal produced such undesirable amounts of smoke and soot (chimneys were unknown in those days), around 1300 King Edward I of England decided to take countermeasures. He made coal burning a crime punishable by death. This solution to the problem turned out to be a bit too drastic and the ban was later lifted. But wood continued to be the primary fuel. By 1700, essentially all of the forests in England had been cut for fuel, and the shift to coal was necessary to avoid extreme hardship.

With the construction of the first steam engine by Newcomen in 1712, coal began to be used as a source of mechanical and, later, electrical power. In 1859, the first producing oil well was opened in northwestern Pennsylvania by Colonel E. A. Drake. Coal, supplemented by oil, furnished the necessary energy to usher in the industrial era. Since these beginnings barely more than a century ago, the use of fossil fuels has been the primary source of energy that has powered the worldwide drive to industrialization. (See Table 4.1.)

TABLE 4.1
Key Episodes in the Development of Energy Sources

ca. 40,000 B.C.	Fire used by Paleolithic man
ca. 3000 B.C.	Use of draft animals
First century B.C.	Waterwheel
Twelfth century A.D.	Vertical windmill
Sixteenth century	Large-scale mining, metallurgical techniques developed
Eighteenth century	Steam engines of Savery (1698), Newcomen (1712), Watt (1765)
Eighteenth to nineteenth centuries	Understanding of the energy concept
Nineteenth century	Formulation of the laws of thermodynamics and electromagnetism
1859	First producing oil well, Titusville, Pennsylvania (Drake)
1876	Internal combustion engine (Otto, Langen)
1882	First steam-generated electric plant, New York City (Edison)
1884	Steam turbine (Parsons)
1892	Diesel engine (Diesel)
1896	First alternating-current hydroelectric plant, Niagara Falls, New York (Westinghouse)
1905	Discovery of relationship between mass and energy (Einstein)
1933	Tennessee Valley Authority (TVA) Act
1942	First self-sustaining nuclear fission chain reaction
1945	First nuclear weapons used, Hiroshima, Nagasaki
1946	Atomic Energy Commission established
1952	First nuclear fusion device (H-bomb), Eniwetok Atoll
1957	First U.S. nuclear power plant devoted exclusively to generating electricity, Shippingport, Pennsylvania
?	First nuclear fusion reactor

In this chapter we examine the sources of energy in use today—water power, fossil fuels, and nuclear fuels—as well as other sources that hold some hope for the future.

THE CHANGING SOURCES OF ENERGY

The ultimate source of almost all of the energy that we use today is in the radiant energy that comes from the Sun. All of our chemical fuels—wood, coal, oil, and natural gas—are derived from plant and animal life that grew because of the action of sunlight. The water that drives hydroelectric generating plants is lifted to high land through evaporation and precipitation processes which result from solar heating. The most important source of energy that is not derived directly from the Sun is stored in nuclei and can be released through fission and fusion. There are also other sources of nonsolar energy but these are of little importance at the present. In this category we find geothermal energy (the source of which is the heat produced in the Earth's interior by radioactivity) and tidal energy (which is due to the relative motion of the Earth and the Moon).

Until about 150 years ago, the primary sources of energy were wood, water, and wind (see Fig. 4.1), plus, of course, the heating effect of the Sun's direct rays. We still make use of these sources, but only water power in the form of electricity generated by huge hydroelectric plants is now a significant factor in the world energy supply. Most of the energy used today is the result of the burning of various chemical fuels (see Table 4.2). The projections for 1985 shown in Table 4.3 indicate that about 50 percent more chemical fuels will be consumed but that the relative proportions will be about the same. Some sectors of the economy depend more on one fuel than on the others. For example, the transportation industry depends almost exclusively on oil products, whereas the electric power industry relies most heavily on coal (see Table 4.4).

TABLE 4.2
Contribution of Various Sources to the Total Energy Consumption in the United States in 1971

Source	Amount	10^{12} kWh	Percentage
Coal	475×10^6 tons	3.7	18.8
Petroleum	5.2×10^9 barrels	8.9	45.2
Natural gas	23×10^{12} ft^3	6.7	34.0
Hydropower		0.3	1.5
Nuclear		0.1	0.5
		19.7	100.0

TABLE 4.3
Contribution of Various Sources to the Estimated Total Energy Consumption in the United States in 1985

Source	Amount	10^{12} kWh	Percentage
Coal	810×10^6 tons	6.3	18.9
Petroleum	8.7×10^9 barrels	14.9	44.7
Natural gas	29×10^{12} ft^3	8.3	25.0
Hydropower		0.4	1.2
Nuclear		3.4	10.2
		33.3	100.0

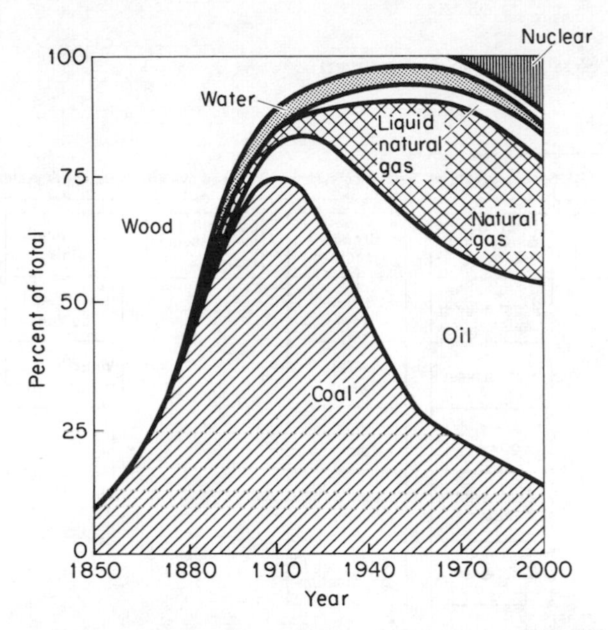

Figure 4.1 Sources of energy in the United States during the period 1850-2000. Notice that the fraction of the total worldwide production of energy by burning coal is now about the same as it was 100 years ago. Even by the year 2000, the impact of the generation of energy by nuclear reactors will be only beginning. [Adapted from Hans H. Landsberg.]

TABLE 4.4
Distribution of Energy Sources According to Use in the United States in 1969[a]

	Residential, commercial	Trans- portation	Industrial	Utilities
Coal	3.1	0.1	24.5	48.3
Natural gas	42.3	4.1	43.4	23.3
Petroleum	38.2	95.7	22.4	10.4
Hydroelectric	—	—	—	17.1
Nuclear	—	—	—	0.9
Electricity purchased	16.4	0.1	9.7	
Total	100.0	100.0	100.0	100.0

[a]All values are percentages.

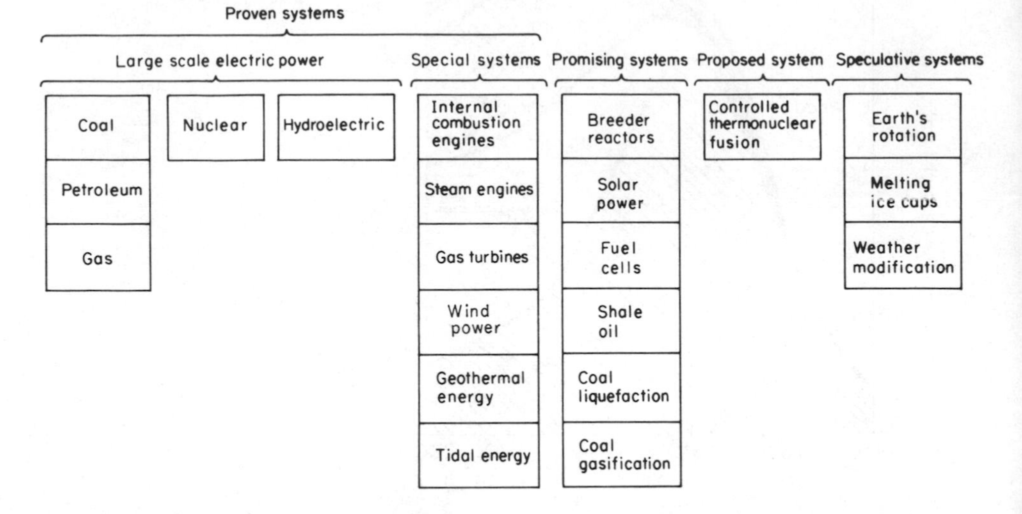

Figure 4.2 Sources of energy. [Adapted from Ali Bulent Cambel.]

In the future an increasing fraction of the world's energy will be obtained from nuclear fission reactors, and hopefully, during the next century, fusion reactors will be available to take over the major burden of energy production. Although the direct use of solar energy (in the form of solar heating and in the generation of electricity) now appears to be a very costly operation, improved techniques may eventually reduce the costs relative to other sources and make solar power an important part of our overall energy picture. Similarly, the widespread use of geothermal energy depends on the development of new technological methods.

Figure 4.2 shows a breakdown of the energy sources currently used and proposed. We discuss many of these sources in the following sections.

WATER POWER

Historically, the utilization of the energy in the flowing water of rivers and streams by means of waterwheels provided the first plentiful and continuous source

Figure 4.3 The hydroelectric generating units of the Wheeler Dam on the Tennessee River. Total generating capacity is 356 MWe in eleven units. [Courtesy of Tennessee Valley Authority.]

of energy. Today, we no longer use water power directly but instead use the potential energy in water stored behind dams to generate electricity. In a modern hydroelectric plant, water is allowed to pass through conduits and drive huge turbines whose rotating shafts are connected to electrical generators (Fig. 4.3).

The largest dams produce electrical power in the range of thousands of megawatts (see Table 4.5). Grand Coulee Dam on the Columbia River in the state of Washington produces about 2000 MWe of electrical power for use in the Northwest; the ultimate capacity of the Grand Coulee plant will be almost 10,000 MWe. At present, the Grand Coulee Dam produces about 0.7 percent of the total electrical energy used in the United States.

TABLE 4.5
The World's Largest Hydroelectric Generating Plants

Name and location	Present power output (MWe)	Ultimate power output (MWe)	Year operational
Grand Coulee, U.S.	2025	9771	1941
Guri, Venezuela	524	6500	1967
Krasnayarsk, U.S.S.R.	5080	6096	1968
Bratsk, U.S.S.R.	4500	4600	1961
Volga, U.S.S.R.	2543	2560	1958
Niagara, U.S.	2190[a]	2400	1961
Volga, U.S.S.R.	2100	2300	1955
Aswan, Egypt	1750	2100	1967
Chief Joseph, U.S.	1024	1950	1961
St. Lawrence, Canada-U.S.	1880	1880	1958
The Dalles, U.S.	1119	1813	1957

[a] Largest hydroelectric generating complex (two plants) now operating in the Western World. Larger plants are under construction in Brazil, Canada, and the United States.

There are 27 major dams on the Tennessee River which were constructed by the Tennessee Valley Authority (TVA) beginning in 1933. The largest of the TVA dams is Wilson Dam in Alabama which produces about one-fourth as much electrical power as Grand Coulee Dam. Since 1950 the hydroelectric power generated by the TVA system has been insufficient to meet the electrical demands of the area, and the Authority has constructed several large coal-fired steam plants to provide supplementary service. In addition, seven TVA-operated nuclear power plants will be in operation within a few years. The total power capacity of the TVA system in 1972 was 20,000 MWe; the expected capacity within a few years will be about 30,000 MWe.

At present (1974), the total installed hydroelectric generating capacity in the United States amounts to about 60,000 MWe. The generating capacity of *all* sources of electrical power is about 460,000 MWe. Altogether, the electrical energy generated in 1971 by hydroelectric plants in the United States was approximately 2.7×10^{11} kWh, which represents about 17 percent of the total electrical energy generated in this country in the same year (1.6×10^{12} kWh). This contribution of hydroelectric energy to the total electrical energy in the United States is quite different from the pattern found in some other countries. For example, in the United Kingdom, with few large rivers, the contribution of hydropower is only 2.3 percent. On the other hand, Brazil obtains more than 80 percent of her electrical energy from hydroelectric sources. In Japan the figure is about 40 percent and in the Soviet Union it is about the same as in the United States (18 percent).

The maximum possible hydropower capacity of the United States has been estimated to be 300,000 MWe (compared to 60,000 MWe already developed). But it is unrealistic to suppose that this maximum figure will ever be reached. There are too many objections to the huge number of dams that would be necessary to approach the ultimate power figure. More reasonably, we might look forward to a doubling of the present capacity to about 120,000 MWe. This situation might be achieved around the year 2000.

The worldwide hydropower resources are estimated to be about 10 times that of the United States—about 3 million megawatts (3×10^6 MWe). Approximately 2.5×10^5 MWe or 8.5 percent of the maximum capacity had been tapped by 1967 (compared to about 20 percent in the United States). The areas with the largest potential are the relatively undeveloped continents—Africa, with 780,000 MWe, and South America, with 577,000 MWe. The worldwide figures are summarized in Table 4.6. It seems possible that a developed capacity of 10^6 MWe could be achieved by the year 2000. This would represent an increase by a factor of 4 over the 1967 capacity.

FOSSIL FUELS

Since the beginning of the twentieth century, most of the world's energy has been derived from the burning of fossil fuels. At the present time less than 10 percent

TABLE 4.6
Worldwide Hydropower Capacities[a]

Region	Potential (MWe)	Percent of total potential	Developed, 1967 (MWe)	Percent developed, 1967
North America	313,000	11	76,000	23
South America	577,000	20	10,000	1.7
Western Europe	158,000	6	90,000	57
Africa	780,000	27	5,000	0.6
Middle East	21,000	1	1,000	4.8
Southeast Asia	455,000	16	6,000	1.3
Far East	42,000	1	20,000	48
Australasia	45,000	2	5,000	11
U.S.S.R., China and satellites	466,000	16	30,000	6.4
Total	2,857,000	100	243,000	8.5

[a]According to M. King Hubbert, 1967.

of the energy used in the United States is obtained from nonfossil sources (see Fig. 4.1). Even though nuclear reactors will supply an increasing fraction of our energy in the future, fossil fuels will continue to be our main source of energy well into the twenty-first century.

Approximately 80 percent of our fossil fuels are used directly, in space heating, in transportation, and in industry; only about 20 percent are used in the generation of electricity. By the year 2000 we will be converting a substantially larger fraction of our fossil fuels (primarily coal) into electrical energy as we shift toward a more electrically oriented economy.

Fossil fuels are produced over long periods of time; but we are using these fuels at a rapid rate. How long can we continue to do this? We have already used approximately 16 percent of the estimated total supplies of oil and natural gas. Fortunately, our supplies of coal are much more extensive; there probably remains 50 times as

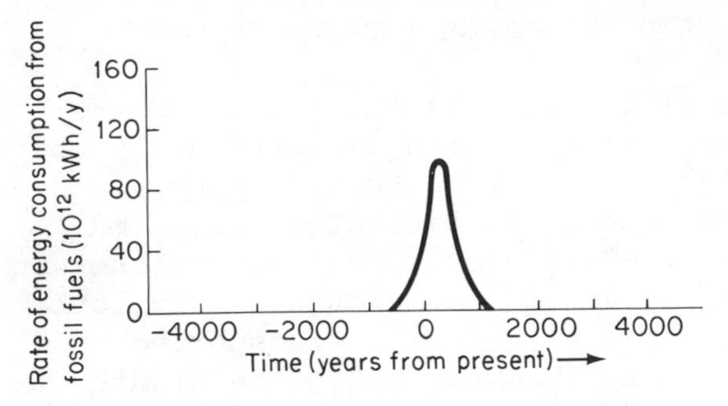

Figure 4.4 Exploitation of fossil fuels during the epoch from 5000 years in the past to 5000 years in the future. [Adapted from M. King Hubbert.]

much coal as has already been mined. Even so, the supply is limited, and at our present rate of consumption, we will exhaust the world's fossil fuel supply within several hundred years.

The high rate of utilization of fossil fuels during the modern era is strikingly illustrated in Fig. 4.4, which shows the rate of energy production from fossil fuels on a time scale that extends from 5000 years in the past to 5000 years in the future. In this diagram, we can see that fossil fuels play an important role only during a brief interval of the world's history. Within 300 or 400 years or so, we will be forced to rely primarily on other sources of energy.

Estimates of this type are necessarily based on the projected status of future technology. If we are successful in devising methods for utilizing low-grade coal and for extracting oil from shale deposits, we may be able to extend the reserves of fossil fuels. But it is clear that it is imperative to develop other nonfossil energy sources. Nuclear reactors, utilizing the fission and fusion processes, or solar power plants must eventually assume the primary burden of supplying the world with energy.

THE FORMATION OF COAL AND PETROLEUM SUBSTANCES

Coal, oil, and natural gas are all the result of the decomposition of living matter. This is immediately obvious from an examination of a piece of coal; under a microscope coal can be seen to contain bits of fossil wood, bark, roots, and leaves. Coal occurs in layers along with sedimentary rocks (mostly shale and sandstone), but unlike sedimentary rocks, coal was not eroded, transported, and deposited—it was formed at the spot where the plants originally grew.

On dry land, dead plant matter (which consists primarily of carbon, hydrogen, and oxygen) decomposes by combining with atmospheric oxygen to form carbon dioxide and water; that is, the plant matter rots away. But in swampy locations, the dead plant matter is covered with water and is therefore protected from the oxidizing action of air. Instead, the plant matter is attacked by anaerobic bacteria. (*Anaerobic bacteria* are bacteria that do not require free oxygen in order to live.) In this process, oxygen and hydrogen escape, and gradually the carbon concentration in the residue becomes higher and higher. The end product of the bacterial action is a soggy carbon-rich substance called *peat*.

Over geological periods of time the peat is covered with an accumulation of sand, silt, and clay. As compression takes place, gases are forced out and the proportion of carbon continues to increase. In this way, the peat is converted into *lignite* and then into *bituminous coal* (see Fig. 4.5). In these forms, coal is a sedimentary rock. The subsequent action of heat and pressure, usually in folded strata, removes even more of the volatile material from the bituminous coal, and produces a metamorphic form of coal called *anthracite*. Lignite and bituminous coal, because they are relatively rich in volatiles, are easy to ignite and burn smokily. Anthracite, on the other hand, contains very little in the way of volatile material, and so is more difficult to ignite but burns with very little smoke. Most of the coal now mined in the eastern United

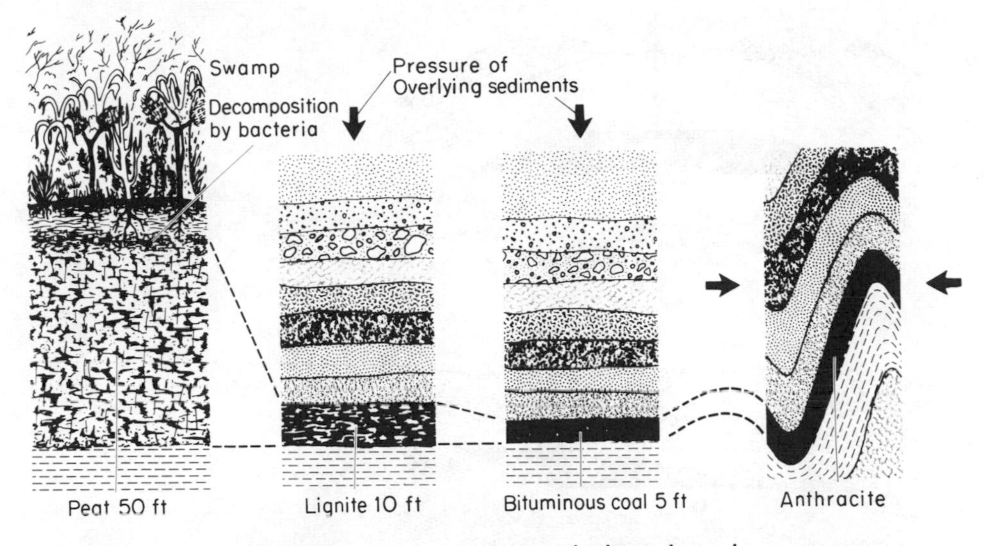

Figure 4.5 Dead plant matter, originating in swampy regions, is converted by bacterial action and compression into lignite and bituminous coal. Additional heat and pressure produce anthracite.

States is bituminous coal, whereas that mined in the western part of the country is mainly lignite or an intermediate grade called sub-bituminous coal.

The process by which oil and natural gas are formed is considerably more complex and less well understood than the events that lead to the formation of coal. Basically, the steps in the creation of oil seem to be the following. The raw material consists mainly of marine organisms, mostly plants, that live near the surface of the sea. When these organisms die and accumulate in basins where the water is stagnant, they are protected from oxidation. As in the case of coal formation, the dead marine matter is decomposed by bacteria. Oxygen, nitrogen, and other elements are removed, leaving mainly carbon and hydrogen. This material is buried by sediment which destroys the bacteria, thus preventing the further decomposition into pure carbon. The accumulating covering layer provides heat and pressure that convert the hydrocarbon material into droplets of liquid oil and bubbles of natural gas.

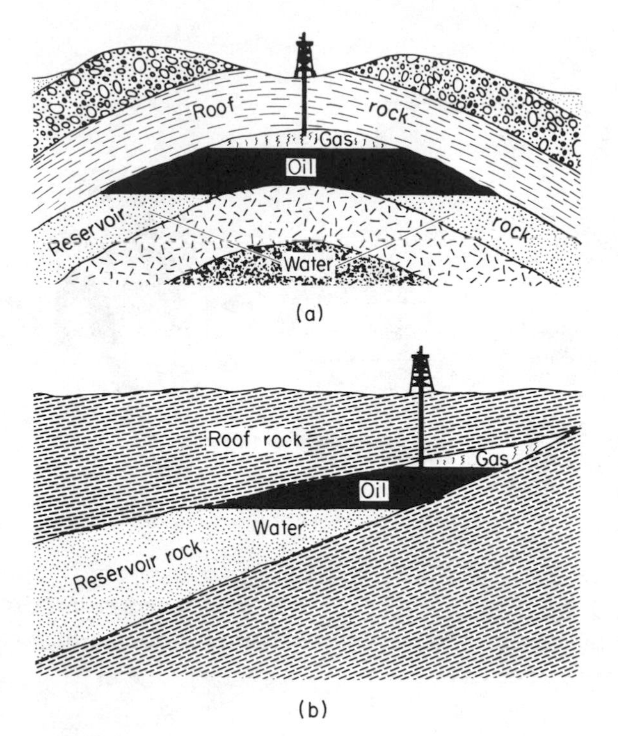

Figure 4.6 Two different types of geologic formation in which oil and gas are found: (a) a structured trap; (b) a stratigraphic trap. The oil is found in porous rock that overlays water-filled rock, the oil and water having separated by the upward migration of the oil.

As additional sedimentary deposits are laid down, the pressure increases and the oil and gas are forced into nearby porous sand or sandstone where the open spaces are larger. Gradually, the oil and gas migrate upward through the sand and they then either escape to the surface or are trapped beneath an impervious roof rock of claystone. This migration process separates the oil from underground water because water molecules readily adhere to sand whereas oil molecules do not. Thus, the oil tends to collect in the pore spaces of sandy rocks beneath roof rocks with the natural gases on top (see Fig. 4.6).

COAL SUPPLIES

Coal is by far our most abundant fuel; deposits occur widely throughout the world. The largest deposits are in the Soviet Union where nearly 60 percent of the world's coal reserves are located. The next largest supply (about 20 percent of the world reserves) is in the United States. Coal has been mined in many parts of this country. There are relatively few anthracite deposits that have been worked (most of which are in Pennsylvania), but bituminous coal is found throughout the central and eastern parts of the country and lignite occurs widely in the northern plains. Most of the coal in the United States lies sufficiently far underground that deep-mining techniques are necessary for its removal. On the other hand, there is enough near-surface coal so that strip mining alone could meet our total coal requirements for many years. (Between 20 and 30 percent of our best coal deposits lie within 100 feet or so of the surface.) Moreover, surface mining can extract 80 to 90 percent of the coal in a deposit, whereas in deep mines about half the coal must be left in place to prevent cave-ins.

Table 4.7 shows the estimated worldwide reserves of coal. The total equivalent energy value of all unmined coal (5.4×10^{16} kWh) indicates that the supply could provide *all* of the energy that the world requires at the present rate of consumption for about 900 years. The United States has sufficient coal to last about 3000 years at our present rate of consumption. Of course, the projected lifespan for coal will change as we alter our rate of usage.

Throughout his history of using coal as a fuel, Man has consumed only about 1.8 percent of the total original supply. Looked at from another viewpoint, millions of years were required to form coal and yet Man seems capable of demolishing the entire supply within less than a thousand years.

TABLE 4.7
Estimated Worldwide Coal Reserves[a]

	Amount (metric tons[b])	Percentage of total	Equivalent energy[c] (kWh)
U.S.S.R.	4.3×10^{12}	56	30.2×10^{15}
United States	1.5×10^{12}	20	10.5×10^{15}
Asia (not including U.S.S.R.)	0.68×10^{12}	9	4.8×10^{15}
North America (not including U.S)	0.60×10^{12}	8	4.2×10^{15}
Western Europe	0.38×10^{12}	5	2.7×10^{15}
Africa	0.11×10^{12}	1	0.8×10^{15}
Australasia	0.06×10^{12}	1 (Australasia and South America combined)	0.4×10^{15}
South America	0.01×10^{12}		0.1×10^{15}
	7.64×10^{12}	100	53.7×10^{15}

[a]According to U.S. Geological Survey, 1971.
[b]1 metric ton = 1000 kg = 2200 lb = 1.1 ton.
[c]Based on an average of 7800 kWh/ton or 7020 kWh/metric ton.

OIL SUPPLIES

Because oil is formed from marine life, oil deposits are widely distributed, especially in coastal areas and beneath the continental shelves (see Fig. 4.7). Oil is also found in inland regions that were once submerged, such as the southwestern and Gulf Coast regions of the United States, the Middle East, and parts of the Sahara desert. The worldwide production of crude oil amounted to more than 17 billion barrels in 1972. Of this, the Middle Eastern countries contributed about 35 percent, and the United States about

Figure 4.7 The petroleum resources that are located beneath the continental shelf are exploited with off-shore drilling equipment such as shown here. [Courtesy of Phillips Petroleum Company.]

20 percent. More than 60 percent of the U.S. production of crude oil is from the states of Texas and Louisiana.

Locating deposits of oil is not as simple as finding minable coal. Coal-bearing layers usually extend over vast areas. Once a coal seam has been located, it can often be followed for many hundreds of miles, and a large number of shafts can be sunk at predictable sites for removing the coal. Similarly, the near-surface layers of coal that are suitable for strip mining can be easily traced over a wide region. Deposits of petroleum tend to be more localized. Even in a proven field, not every well that is drilled will yield oil. The search for oil is therefore much more uncertain than locating sites of minable coal. In recent years, explorations have uncovered several large deposits of oil—for example, in the North Sea, on the North Slope of Alaska, and off the shore of Southeast Asia.

Because of the generally predictable nature of coal deposits, geologists have been able to make what are considered to be quite reliable estimates of coal reserves. But estimating oil reserves is a much more difficult task. The great uncertainties in oil reserve figures was brought out clearly in the Congressional hearings in early 1974.

In discussing petroleum reserves, we must distinguish between two types of "reserves." One is the *proved reserve*, which represents oil deposits that are currently being worked or that we are confident can be exploited. In addition, there are regions from which oil can probably be recovered, and others where future discoveries are likely to be made (for example, beneath the ocean floors). Taken together, these various categories represent the *estimated ultimate recovery* figures. Table 4.8 shows both sets of figures for liquid petroleum reserves.

The figures listed in Table 4.8 represent the results of only one of the many studies of the petroleum reserve situation. Other estimates range from 38×10^9 barrels for the U.S. proved reserves to more than 400×10^9 barrels for the U.S. ultimate recovery figure.

If the present worldwide rate of oil consumption (17×10^9 barrels per year) were to remain constant, the proved reserves of 672×10^9 barrels (Table 4.8) represent only a 40-year supply. Actually, because of the increasing rate of using petroleum, the expected lifetime of these reserves is even shorter. Undoubtedly, new fields will be opened in the future, and we will tap to a greater and greater extent the "ultimate recovery" reserves. Recent explorations have shown that the continental shelves contain more—perhaps much more—liquid petroleum than previously suspected. In spite of the high costs of developing these deposits, we can expect a much higher activity in offshore drilling during the coming years. It therefore

TABLE 4.8

Estimated Worldwide Liquid Petroleum Reserves

Region	Proved reserves[a] (billions of barrels)	Estimated ultimate recovery[b] (proved + probable + future discoveries)		
		Amount (billions of barrels)	Percentage of total	Equivalent energy (kWh)[c]
Middle East	355	600	29	10.2×10^{14}
U.S.S.R. and China	98	500	24	8.5×10^{14}
Africa	106	250	12	4.2×10^{14}
Latin America	17	225	11	3.8×10^{14}
United States	43[d]	200[d]	9.5	3.4×10^{14}
Far East	15	200	9.5	3.4×10^{14}
Canada	25	95	4	1.6×10^{14}
Europe	13	20[e]	1	0.3×10^{14}
Total world	672	2090	100	35.4×10^{14}

[a]According to Hussein K. Abdel-Aar (1972 figures).

[b]According to W. P. Ryman (1967 figures).

[c]Based on 1700 kWh per 42-gal barrel.

[d]These figures are certainly low due to more recent exploration and development of the Alaskan North Slope field and offshore deposits. The total U.S. ultimate recovery figure probably exceeds 400 billion barrels.

[e]Does not reflect the full extent of the North Sea fields, which are still being explored and developed.

seems reasonable to expect that we will have adequate petroleum stocks at our disposal beginning within a few years, after the present shortages have been corrected, and extending well into the next century.

THE PROCESSING OF PETROLEUM

Coal (which is essentially pure carbon) and natural gas (which is primarily methane) can both be used directly as fuels without further processing. On the other hand, petroleum in the form of crude oil is not directly useful. Crude oil consists of a variety of hydrocarbon compounds which can be separated by a process called *fractional distillation*. (This process is based on the fact that the different hydrocarbon compounds have different boiling points.) About 50 percent of a typical crude oil can be separated by fractional distillation into compounds that are suitable for the preparation of gasoline. These compounds consist of long-chain hydrocarbon molecules, ranging from C_6H_{14} (hexane) to $C_{10}H_{22}$ (decane). The longer-chain compounds have boiling points that are too high for incorporation into gasoline, although they are used in kerosene, fuel oils, and lubricating oils.

The longer-chain hydrocarbons can be broken down into smaller molecules suitable for fuels by a processing called *cracking*. Fractional distillation and cracking are carried out in huge refinery complexes that are usually located near the sources of the crude oil (for example, in Texas, Louisiana, Oklahoma, and California) or near ports where the crude oil is brought by tankers (for example, in New Jersey). One of the factors that has aggravated the recent fuel shortage is the inadequacy of our refinery capacity to meet the current demand. When gasoline supplies became short during the summer of 1973, some refinery capacity was diverted from the preparation of heating oil to the manufacture of gasoline. Because the refineries could not then meet the schedule of heating oil deliveries, these fuels were in short supply during the winter months.

TABLE 4.9
Uses of Petroleum

Use	Percentage
Transportation	52.9
Residential and commercial	17.7
Industrial	11.6
Nonenergy	10.6
Electrical generation	7.2
	100.0

Inadequate refinery capacity will be a problem well into the future. Large capital investments and long lead-times are required for the construction of refineries. We will need 35 new refineries (each with a capacity of 160,000 barrels per day) by 1980, and 60 by 1985. Even if we increase domestic production of crude oil and if we are able to negotiate increased imports, we are likely to be short of refinery capacity for several years. One of the major problems faced by oil companies wishing to construct new refineries is finding suitable sites. Who wants an oil refinery in his backyard?

As shown in Table 4.9, the major use of petroleum is in the preparation of fuels for transportation. Notice, however, that more than 10 percent of our petroleum is used for "nonenergy" purposes. These include the preparation of asphalt, lubricants, and waxes of various sorts. In addition, petroleum (and to a lesser extent, coal and natural gas) is the raw material for the huge petrochemical industry. More than 75 million tons of petrochemicals are produced worldwide each year.

Many of our modern substances are carbon-containing compounds based on petroleum hydrocarbons. Among these are synthetic rubber, artificial fibers of various types, polyethylene, Styrofoam, polyurethane, and a long list of other "plastics." One of the important starting materials used in the manufacture of many of these products is *ethylene*, C_2H_4. Ethylene is produced by the cracking of long-chain petroleum hydrocarbons.

Because petroleum supplies are essential to the petrochemical industry, any oil shortage automatically means a shortage in petroleum-based products. Whenever gasoline and heating oil become scarce, you can also look toward shortages in synthetic insulating materials, plastic wrapping materials, and automobile tires.

NATURAL GAS SUPPLIES

Natural gas is the cleanest burning of the fossil fuels (and, because of government regulation, also the least expensive at the present time). Therefore, natural gas is in great demand, particularly for space heating. By 1970, the demand for natural gas in the United States had exceeded the capacity of the domestic suppliers. Imports of natural gas are now steadily increasing, and domestic production is expected to peak in 1975 and thereafter to decrease. Between 1974 and 1985, it is expected that the demand for natural gas in the United States will increase by about 60 percent. But the total available supplies, including imports, will probably remain approximately constant. We are therefore faced with an increasing demand deficit, or "gas gap."

Generally, liquid petroleum and natural gas occur together in underground deposits (see Fig. 4.6). As we have brought more and more petroleum to the surface, we have also tapped new sources of natural gas. In recent years, the yield of natural gas has been reasonably constant at about 6000 ft^3 per barrel of oil. If we consider the proven U.S. oil reserves, not including Alaska, of 43×10^9 barrels (see Table 4.8), then the corresponding reserves of natural gas amount to $6000 \times (43 \times 10^9)$ or 258×10^{12} ft^3. In 1973, the U.S. consumption of natural gas was 26×10^{12} ft^3. Our present domestic reserves, not including any allowance for imports, represent a 10-year supply at the current rate of consumption. If we take the optimistic view and consider an ultimate recovery figure for oil, including Alaska, of 400×10^9 barrels, the natural gas lifetime increases to 92 years. (Remember, these lifetime figures are based on the present consumption rate and must actually be substantially reduced because of the anticipated increase in demand for natural gas.)

It has been suggested that we can stimulate gas fields to yield greater amounts of natural gas. If the gas is trapped in sandstone layers, it often does not escape easily even if it is directly tapped. In 1973, the U.S. Atomic Energy Commission detonated three atomic weapons devices more than a mile beneath Colorado's Western Slope in an effort to release a large quantity of trapped natural gas (Project Rio Blanco). As shown in Fig. 4.8, the explosion created a long cylindrical cavity which penetrates several layers of gas-bearing sandstone. Gas is expected to seep into the cavity for 20 years or more, producing at least 20 billion cubic feet of usable natural gas.

Even though the Rio Blanco experiment was successful, it seems unlikely that natural gas released by the detonation of atomic weapons will provide any substantial fraction of our future natural gas requirements. The amount of gas released by the Rio Blanco explosion represents only about 0.1 percent of the gas that is used in the United States each year. It is totally unrealistic to expect that we will embark on a campaign to explode thousands of atomic devices each year in order to increase gas production.

Beginning in the late 1960s, we began to import natural gas, primarily from the North African fields. Within a few years, we will be importing Soviet gas. Domestically produced natural gas can easily be distributed to users through the extensive pipeline system that exists in this country. But how do we handle bulky shipments of gas from overseas supplies? Because 625 ft^3 of natural gas occupies only 1 ft^3 in the liquid state, there is a substantial savings in space if the gas is shipped as liquefied natural gas (LNG). Natural gas is mainly the hydrocarbon *methane*, CH_4. This gas will not liquefy under pressure unless the temperature is very low. The usual condition at which LNG is transported is a pressure of

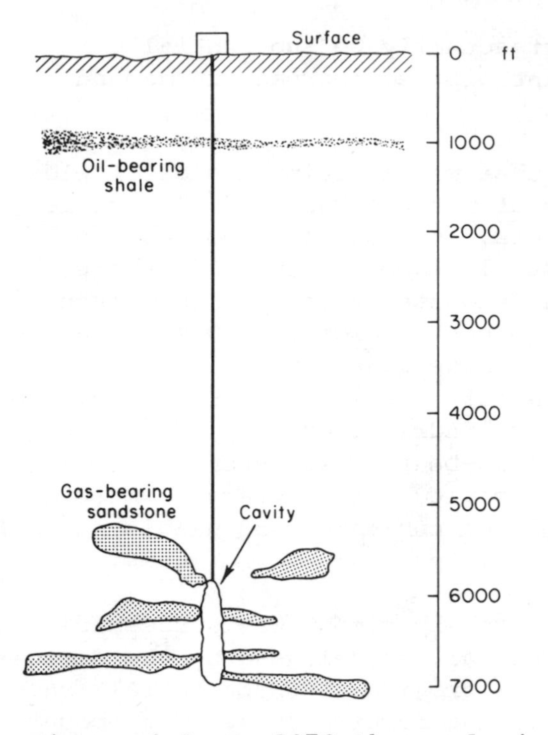

Figure 4.8 In 1973 the explosion of three atomic weapons devices created a cavity more than a mile beneath the surface into which natural gas will seep for 20 years or more (Project Rio Blanco).

several hundred pounds per square inch (15 lb/in.^{2} is normal atmospheric pressure) and a temperature of about -260°F. The over-ocean transport of LNG from foreign gas fields, therefore, requires special cryogenic or "thermos bottle" tankers. The few tankers now equipped for such service are capable of carrying about a billion cubic feet (10^9 ft^3) of natural gas in liquid form. Newer models will have almost 3 times the capacity and will be about the size of a 250,000-ton oil tanker. It is anticipated that a fleet of 100 to 150 such tankers will be needed to handle our LNG imports by 1985.

ALTERNATE SOURCES OF LIQUID PETROLEUM

The supplies of liquid petroleum and natural gas are rapidly being depleted toward levels that we can only classify as precarious. Clearly, corrective action must be taken as quickly as possible. We have already seen that stimulation of natural gas fields is not a realistic prospect. However, the stimulation of oil fields (by nonexplosive means) does seem feasible. In most oil field operations, only about 30 percent of the total amount of oil in the field is actually removed. Techniques are being developed to increase substantially the fraction of yield. For example, if water is pumped down an oil well, the water will flood some of the spaces occupied by the untapped oil, thereby forcing oil to a higher level, from which it can be recovered by pumping from a nearby well. It is anticipated that these *secondary recovery* techniques will permit the removal of an additional 30 percent of the total amount of oil in many fields.

Petroleum compounds are found not only in underground pools of liquid crude oil but also in certain types of solid rock. In some regions hydrocarbons are trapped in fine-grained rocks called *shale*. Extensive deposits of high-grade oil-bearing shale are known in Colorado, Utah, and Wyoming. Lower-grade deposits cover much of the central United States, extending from Texas to Pennsylvania. There are probably more than 600×10^9 barrels of oil in shale that contains at least 25 gallons per ton. It has been estimated that there is about 1000 times as much hydrocarbon material in oil shales as in crude oil throughout the world. Extracting useful fuel from oil shales poses a variety of special problems which have not yet been solved. At the present time only about 0.01 percent of the known oil shale deposits are classified as "recoverable" and are listed as part of the useful reserves. If methods can be devised to extract fuels from these shales in an efficient manner, the world's useful reserves of fossil fuels will increase enormously.

As mentioned in Chapter 1, some of the newly available research and development funds will be used to investigate methods for recovering shale oil. Basically, the oil is removed from the shale by heating it to about 800°C. One proposal is to heat the shale *in situ* so that the standard mining operation is bypassed. Apart from the technical difficulties in the extraction of oil from the shale, there are severe environmental problems as well. Any practical process will require enormous amounts of water. Where will adequate supplies be found? The areas in which the best shale deposits occur have no oversupply of water. What can be done with the huge amounts of slag that will remain after the processing? And what will become of the land? Can it be restored and used for some purpose? These are formidable problems; but the potential supply of fuel is so great that a concentrated effort is already under way to overcome the difficulties.

Although it represents a smaller ultimate supply, the oil contained in *tar sands* is probably the most available and least expensive new source of petroleum. The largest deposits of this type are in Canada, where there are an estimated 300×10^9 barrels in the Athabasca tar sands, 80×10^9 barrels of which are recoverable by methods now in use. A small recovery plant (65,000 barrels per day) has been in operation since 1967. Because of the steadily increasing cost of pool crude oil (the price of North African and Middle East crude oil has more than tripled in the last year or so), it is now economically feasible to enlarge the tar sands operations.

COAL GASIFICATION AND LIQUEFACTION

The most promising long-term prospect for extending the lifetime of our petroleum and natural gas supplies is through the use of *coal*. Coal is our most abundant chemical fuel. And yet, as shown in Table 4.2, the burning of coal produces only about 19 percent of the energy we now derive from fossil fuels. As liquid petroleum and natural gas become short in supply, we must turn again to coal as a major source of energy. We can do this in two ways. First, we can use more coal in the production of electricity. Many of the coal-fired generating plants—especially those in the Eastern United States—have been converted to use oil as the fuel. This change was made because of the easy availability of oil from North Africa and the Middle East, and because air pollution standards are easier to meet with oil than with the high-sulfur coals of the Eastern United States. Although the uncontrolled burning of coal does produce large quantities of fly ash and noxious gases, these emissions can be substantially eliminated using modern techniques. The installation of control devices will be a contributing factor in the increasing cost of energy usage.

Second, the carbon in coal can be converted into gaseous and liquid hydrocarbons that can be substituted for natural gas and liquid petroleum products. In the *Fischer-Tropsch* process, for example, coal (carbon) and steam at about 600°C are converted into carbon monoxide:

$$C + H_2O \xrightarrow{600°C} CO + H_2 \qquad (4.1)$$

The $CO + H_2$ mixture (called *water gas*) is enriched with additional hydrogen and then passed over a catalyst (cobalt plus thorium dioxide) at a temperature of about 250°C. This produces a mixture of hydrocarbons which can be separated by collecting each compound at its characteristic boiling temperature (fractional distillation). For example, the reaction which produces pentane is

$$5\ CO + 11\ H_2 \longrightarrow \underset{\text{pentane}}{C_5H_{12}} + 5\ H_2O \qquad (4.2)$$

At a large processing plant, coal can be converted into clean-burning hydrocarbons using techniques that effectively control the undesirable products of coal burning, namely, fly ash and noxious gases such as sulfur dioxide. Again, the solution to the problem is expensive. It has been estimated that a capital investment of $4 to $5 billion would be required to construct gasification plants with an annual capacity of 10^{12} ft^3, or less than 5 percent of our national demand. Gasified coal is a high-cost fuel.

Synthetic natural gas (SNG) can also be prepared from liquid petroleum compounds. But this does not assist in preserving our petroleum supplies, and SNG prepared from petroleum is no cheaper than SNG prepared from coal. The current cost of natural gas to a user in New York City is about $0.45 per thousand cubic feet. The cost of SNG (whether prepared from coal or from liquid petroleum) is about 3 times greater.

One of the most exciting prospects for coal gasification is to make the conversion to gas *in situ*. That is, instead of bringing the coal to the surface by conventional mining techniques, the gasification process is carried out using underground, unmined coal. The gas is then piped to the surface and transported to the ultimate consumer. Although a pilot plant for *in situ* coal gasification has not yet been constructed, the idea appears to be feasible and offers the possibility of bypassing some of the more troublesome steps in the utilization of coal.

The conclusion that we must draw from this discussion of the fossil fuel situation is that we are being forced once again to turn to coal as our primary energy source. And this coal-based economy will persist until breeder reactors, or nuclear fusion reactors, or solar power systems are brought into operation on a large scale.

Although we may be able to meet our near-term energy requirements through increased reliance on coal, the prospect is not a happy one from many viewpoints. First, it will be much more expensive to use coal in the future than it has been in the past. Mining costs are higher, elaborate equipment is required to eliminate noxious gases and smoke in the burning process, and gasification is a costly operation. Second, there will be a huge price to pay in terms of environmental effects. The mining of coal, whether by deep mining through shafts or by strip mining, uses up enormous chunks of real estate. Land use, air quality, and water quality are all affected in an adverse way by extracting coal from the earth. (We discuss the environmental problems associated with energy usage in Chapter 7.) Every effort to minimize these effects increases the cost of the energy we use. At what point will energy usage (that is, our standard of living) and environmental quality finally come into equilibrium?

NUCLEAR FUEL

The most concentrated form of energy that is available to Man is stored in nuclei. This energy can be released in the processes of *fission* (the splitting apart of heavy nuclei) and *fusion* (the fusing together of light nuclei). We discuss both of these types of reactions in the next chapter. Fission reactors have been producing electricity in commercial quantities for only about 20 years (see Table 4.1). But as our reserves of fossil fuels are depleted, nuclear power plants will almost certainly continue to supply a larger and larger fraction of the energy we use. In the United States in 1968, for example, the usage of nuclear-generated electricity amounted to about 900 kWh per person. By the year 2000, it is estimated that this figure will increase to 35,000 kWh per person (and during the same period, the population will increase by 50 percent from 200 million to 300 million). Although we may continue to use fossil fuels for certain purposes (particularly for transportation and in the petrochemical industry), it is most likely that, by the middle of the twenty-first century, we will be generating electricity almost exclusively from nuclear power plants (unless some major breakthrough is made in solar power generating systems). These nuclear plants will use uranium and thorium in fission reactions, and when a feasible fusion reactor has been developed, heavy hydrogen (*deuterium*) and lithium will probably become the principal fuels.

The energy available in a given mass of nuclear fuel is several *million* times greater than in the same mass of a fossil fuel. For example, the fission energy contained in 1 kg of uranium is the same as that contained in 3.4×10^6 kg of coal. A total of about 10 billion tons of coal would be required to produce enough energy to meet the annual worldwide needs, whereas only 3000 tons of uranium could produce the same amount of energy.

The situation at present, however, is not nearly this attractive. There are three major factors that increase the amount of uranium necessary to produce a given number of kilowatt-hours of electrical energy:

1. Present-day reactors use uranium-235 (^{235}U) which has an abundance of only 0.7 percent in naturally occurring uranium.

2. Only about 2 percent of the theoretical maximum available fission energy is actually extracted from the uranium fuel elements used in today's reactors.

3. The efficiency of converting fission energy into electrical energy in present-day reactors is about 32 percent.

In conventional ^{235}U reactors, there is only slight room for improvement. By recycling the uranium that remains in used fuel elements, the efficiency of extracting fission energy can be increased to about 3 percent. New designs for the cooling systems in reactors will increase the electrical efficiency from 32 percent to about 40 percent (which is the efficiency of coal-fired power plants).

The really striking improvement in efficiency will come when the new *breeder* reactors become operational. These reactors will generate power and, at the same time, will "breed" new fuel from plentiful ^{238}U or thorium (^{232}Th). In fact, these reactors will produce more fissionable fuel than they use. We return to the discussion of breeder reactors in the next chapter. For now, we need only note that breeder reactors could conceivably produce all of the energy required by the world at present (6×10^{13} kWh/year) by consuming only about 9000 tons of uranium and thorium metal each year.

Uranium and thorium do not occur isolated in rich deposits as do coal and oil. First of all, these elements usually are found as oxide ores: U_3O_8 (uranium oxide) and ThO_2 (thorium oxide). Second, the ores occur in small concentrations mixed among various kinds of rocky material. The lower the concentration of the ore, the more expensive is the extraction process. Because of the importance of nuclear fuels in weapons, figures are not available for the reserves in Communist countries. In the non-Communist world it has been estimated that there are about a million tons of uranium oxide that can be mined at a cost of $10 per pound; about half of this amount is in the United States and Canada. In order to meet future requirements, another million tons of uranium ore will have to be discovered and developed by 1985.

For the long term, it will be necessary to tap low-grade ores for our supplies of nuclear fuels. Both uranium and thorium are relatively abundant elements; they occur widely in low concentrations in a variety of different rocky materials. Beneath large areas of Tennessee, Kentucky, Ohio, Indiana, and Illinois there lies, at minable depths, a 5-m-thick layer of *Chattanooga black shale*. This shale contains about 0.15 kg of uranium per cubic meter. A column of shale 1 m^2 in area and 5 m thick contains nuclear fuel equivalent to 2000 metric tons of coal. An area of 16 km by 16 km would yield an amount of nuclear energy equal to that of the entire world's ultimate-recovery petroleum reserves (3.5×10^{15} kWh).

A similar situation exists for thorium. In addition to high-grade ores of thorium which are about as abundant as those of uranium, there are many regions of extensive low-grade deposits. The *Conway Granite* in New Hampshire, for example, contains about 0.15 kg of thorium per cubic meter. This deposit covers an area of about 750 km^2 and is probably a few kilometers in depth. If the entire area were quarried to a depth of 100 m, the energy equivalent of the thorium would be about 2×10^{15} kWh, sufficient to supply the United States with all of its energy needs at the present rate for 100 years.

It should be emphasized that the utilization of low-grade uranium and thorium ores assumes the development of a system of breeder-reactor power stations. Several breeder reactors have been constructed, but at present only one (in the Soviet Union) is producing commercial quantities of electricity. It will be a decade or more before any substantial number of breeder reactors are brought on-line in the United States.

The fuel supply picture for fusion power is extremely attractive. The primary fuel will be deuterium (or *heavy hydrogen*, ^2H) or, in some of the proposed systems, deuterium plus lithium. The world's oceans constitute a huge source of deuterium in the form of water—about one molecule of every 3000 water molecules contains an atom of deuterium. The deuterium in 1 m^3 of water has an energy equivalent equal to that of 300 metric tons of coal. There are about 1.4×10^{18} m^3 of water in the oceans, with an energy equivalent of more than 10^{24} kWh. If we can succeed in the development of a practical source of fusion power, then Mankind is assured of a plentiful supply of energy for millennia!

In the next chapter we discuss some of the technical difficulties associated with the development of fusion power and the realization of the dream of an eternal supply of energy.

GEOTHERMAL ENERGY

The interior of the Earth is extremely hot—so hot, in fact, that the central core consists of molten iron. From a temperature of about 20°C at the surface of the Earth, there is an increase to about 1000°C at a depth of only 40 km. Even for the relatively shallow penetrations of mine shafts, the temperature increases are substantial and limit the depths at which miners can work. Molten rock, liquefied at the extreme temperatures beneath the Earth's crust, is forced to the surface through cracks and fissures and is ejected in the form of lava from volcanoes. Hot water and steam are similarly released at the Earth's surface from hot springs and geysers. It has been estimated that there are 700,000,000 km^3 of superheated water (temperature about 200°C) beneath the Earth's surface. All of this heated material—rocks, steam, and water—represents an enormous reservoir of energy.

Figure 4.9 The Geysers generating plant, near San Francisco, is the largest station in the world for producing electricity from geothermal energy. [Courtesy of Pacific Gas and Electric Company.]

As long ago as 1904, engineers in Larderello, Italy tapped the supply of geothermal energy by drilling special wells into the underground steam supply. This natural steam drives electricity-producing turbines, and now the Larderello plant generates 390 MWe of power. Other geothermal systems are in operation in New Zealand, the Soviet Union, Japan, Iceland, Mexico, and Kenya. At the Geysers, 90 miles north of San Francisco, steam wells drive generators that supply 300 MWe of electrical power (Fig. 4.9). The ultimate capacity of this facility is estimated to be in the range of 1000 to 4000 MWe. According to one estimate there is sufficient hot brine beneath the Imperial Valley in California to produce 20,000 MWt for a century.

Although at first glance they may seem to represent an ideal form of natural power, geothermal sources are far from being trouble free and without pollution. Even the purest underground steam contains enough hydrogen sulfide (with its characteristic odor of rotten eggs) to be extremely unpleasant and enough minerals to poison fish and other forms of marine life in streams and rivers into which the condensed steam is discharged. Furthermore, the removal of underground steam and water causes the surface to subside. In one Mexican steam field, for example, the subsidence has already amounted to about 5 inches. Some of the difficulties attending the utilization of geothermal power can be overcome if the condensed steam is pumped back underground, but such measures are not yet in general use.

Of even greater potential than underground steam and heated water is the heat energy stored in subsurface rocks. Some of this energy could be recovered and used by pumping water into the region by means of deep wells. Upon being pumped back to the surface, the heated water could be utilized to drive electrical generators in the same way that natural underground hot water is used. Although there is probably 10 times as much energy that could be recovered from heated rocks than is available from natural steam and hot water (a potential of about 600,000 MWe), no plants have yet been constructed to tap this energy source. Scientists are now studying a 2-mile by 5-mile region near Marysville, Montana, where rock at 500°C lies only a mile below the surface. This relatively small source has the potential of supplying 10 percent of the U.S. electrical needs for 30 years.

There is a sufficient number of potential geothermal sites in the world that, with vigorous development, could represent a significant energy resource. Geothermal energy will not, at least in the near future, replace the major energy sources now being used. But it has been estimated that, by the end of this century, the United States could be producing 100,000 MWe of geothermal electrical power. This figure represents about 10 percent of the projected electrical power requirements of the

United States in the year 2000. (An optimistic estimate places the geothermal generating capacity at 395,000 MWe by the end of the century.)

TIDAL POWER

It is possible to extract energy from water in ways other than the damming of rivers. For example, in certain parts of the world tides rise to prodigious heights. On the coasts of Nova Scotia and Brittany (in northern France), and in the Gulfs of Alaska and Siam, the tidal variations amount to 40 feet or more. This twice daily surging of water back and forth in narrow channels represents a potential source of power. Although not of major significance on a worldwide scale, tidal power should be useful in particular areas. The first tidal-powered electric generating plant is on the Rance River in France and is harnessing the power of the English Channel tides which rise to as much as 44 feet at this location (Fig. 4.10). By opening gates as the tide rises and then closing them at high tide, a 9-square-mile pool is formed behind the Rance River Dam. As the tide lowers, the trapped water is allowed to flow out, driving 24 electricity-generating turbines of 13 MWe capacity each for a total average power output of 310 MWe. A project begun in 1934 for the development of tidal power at Passamaquoddy Bay between Maine and Canada has now been abandoned as uneconomical. (Instead, it appears that the Passamaquoddy Bay area will be the site of a new oil refinery complex.) Other potential tidal power sites are Cook Inlet in Alaska, San José Gulf in Argentina, and a location on the White Sea near Murmansk in the Soviet Union. The total world potential for tidal power has been estimated to be about 2×10^6 MWe. Although this represents an important energy source in certain localities, the amount is insufficient to make a major impact on the world's energy supply.

Figure 4.10 The Rance River tidal generating plant, shown here under construction in 1965. The plant now produces a peak power of about 300 MWe. [Phototheque EDF, Michel Brigand.]

ELECTRICITY FROM SOLAR RADIATION

The source of energy most readily available to us is sunlight. At the top of the atmosphere, solar energy is incident at an average rate of approximately 1.4 kW/m^2. The total amount of energy received by the Earth from the Sun in a year amounts to 1.6×10^{18} kWh. Because of absorption in the atmosphere and reflection from clouds, only about half of the incident energy reaches the surface of the Earth, and averaged over a day, the solar power is about 0.2 kW/m^2.

If we could find a way to make efficient use of solar energy, we would have a continuing "free" supply of energy which would not degrade our environment and which would lift at least a portion of the burden on our nonrenewable fuel supplies. The primary problem associated with utilizing solar energy is that the energy is spread thinly over the Earth and is variable due to local weather conditions and the regular day-night cycle. In the relatively cloudless desert regions of the southwestern United States, for example, the rate at which solar energy reaches the Earth's surface during the 6 to 8 hours around mid-day is about 0.8 kW/m^2. The energy absorbed per square meter per year amounts to about 2000 kWh.

The second problem is that only a small fraction of the absorbed solar energy can actually be converted into electrical energy. Estimates of the conversion efficiency for proposed systems are about 10 percent. That is, the annual absorbed solar energy per square meter on the surface of the Earth represents about 200 kWh of electrical energy under favorable weather conditions. (We discuss solar *heating* in the next section.)

A modern electrical generating plant operating at a power level of 1000 MWe could produce about 9×10^9 kWh of electrical energy per year (if operated continuously at peak capacity). In order to duplicate this figure, an area of 45×10^6 m^2 would have to be covered with solar energy converters. This "solar farm" would be about 7 km by 7 km. In order to meet the total demand for electrical energy in the United States in the year 2000, the area covered by solar farms would amount to more than 5000 km^2, about 0.16 percent of the surface area of the United States.

Any solar farm that is capable of competing with conventional power plants in the production of electricity will necessarily be very large—and it will be expensive. A nuclear power plant (1000 MWe) costs about $500,000,000, and a coal-fired plant costs about half as much. But a 1000-MWe solar farm would probably cost several times more than a nuclear plant. The projected cost of electricity delivered by a solar farm is 3 to 4 times more than today's cost for electricity from nuclear and fossil-fuel power plants. Thus the utilization of solar energy on a wide scale is not now economically feasible.

One of the major problems associated with the development of solar farms to generate electricity is the high cost of the converter elements or *solar cells*. The best and most efficient solar cells are constructed from high-purity silicon. This is the type of cell that has been used so successfully in the space program to provide electrical power in spacecraft. At the present time, silicon converters cost about $300 per watt of electrical output. This cost would have to be reduced to about $1 per watt before the construction of a silicon-cell solar farm would be practical. Moreover, a 1000-MWe solar farm would require about 30×10^6 kg of silicon; this figure represents about 60 times the present annual production of high-purity silicon in the United States. It is conceivable that increased production, coupled with new purification techniques, could substantially lower the material costs and provide sufficient converters for a solar farm. In addition, it might be possible to use other less efficient but cheaper materials, such as cadmium sulfide.

Solar cells convert sunlight directly into electrical power. In another scheme for the utilization of solar energy, sunlight is concentrated by lenses and is used to heat an absorbing material located within a system of pipes. Nitrogen or helium gas flowing through the pipes transfers the heat to a central storage unit. This heat is then used to drive steam turbines for the production of electrical power. Because the performance of most of the materials that could be used as absorbers suffers severely at elevated temperatures, power plants using this scheme would necessarily operate at relatively low temperatures with a consequent reduction in efficiency. The cost of such a system is high and the durability of the components in long-term operation is a major concern.

The prospects for the large-scale production of electrical power from sunlight do not now appear bright. But as the costs of conventional fuels rise, as construction becomes more expensive for conventional facilities, and as more environmental controls are required, solar energy may appear as a viable alternative to conventional sources of energy. A recent study has indicated that within 50 years or so, solar energy could provide more than 20 percent of the electrical power requirements of the United States. Thus, it seems that for many years, solar farms can be no more than backup systems for conventional and nuclear power plants.

SOLAR HEATING

Although it appears that the large-scale generation of electricity from solar radiation is at best many years in the future, the heating (and cooling) of homes and businesses with the Sun's rays may become widespread within a much shorter time. By 1973, only a few dozen homes in the United States had been constructed with solar heating systems. But as fuel costs rise and increasing emphasis is placed on "clean" energy, it seems probable that more and more new construction will incorporate some sort of arrangement for the utilization of solar radiation. It has been estimated that in the next 5 to 10 years, perhaps 10 percent of the new homes will be at least partially heated by solar radiation.

One type of home solar heating system is shown schematically in Fig. 4.11. Solar radiation is incident on a collector which is placed on the south-facing slope of the roof. Water in the transfer loop is heated and is pumped to the heat reservoir (also water) which receives a portion of the heat. When heat is required in the house (as sensed by a thermostat), warm water from the heat reservoir is pumped through a coil in the heating duct. A fan forces warm air throughout the house. If the water temperature in the reservoir is not sufficiently high to provide adequate heating, an auxiliary supply adds heat to the reservoir water.

During extremely cold weather, especially on sunless days, a large amount of auxiliary heating will be required. Therefore, in a typical installation, an average of only about one-third to one-half of the necessary heating could be supplied by solar radiation. Solar heating therefore

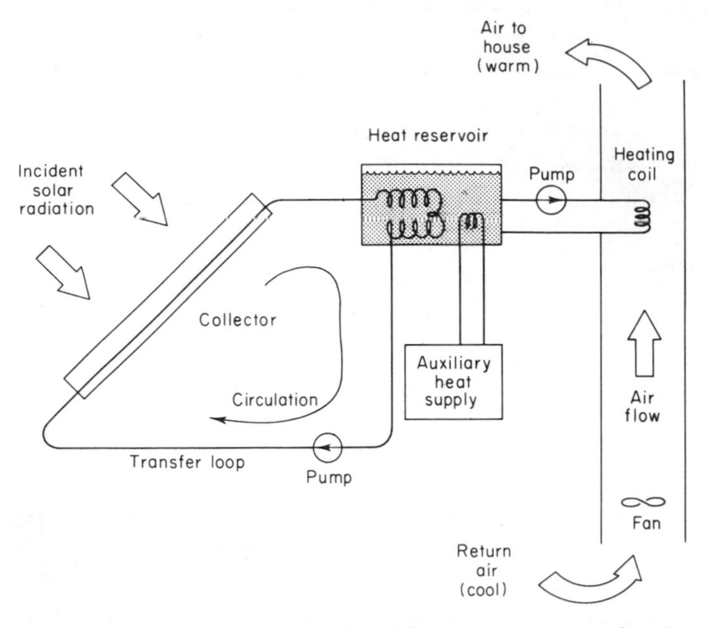

Figure 4.11 Schematic diagram of a simple home solar heating system.

offers the possibility of substantial savings in fuel costs. But it must be remembered that these savings come only at the price of increased construction costs. According to some estimates, the special equipment required for an effective solar heating system may add up to 10 percent to the construction cost for a new house. In order to offer real economic advantages to a homeowner, it will be necessary to install a more complex system, one that provides *cooling* as well as *heating*. It is this type of solar heating-cooling system that the experts envisage coming into the new construction market in substantial quantities within a few years. Perhaps 10 percent of the new homes will be so equipped. The resulting impact on total fuel consumption will not be large, but it will provide a useful saving. The most significant effect of home solar systems will be to relieve the peak-load situations that occur in hot weather when everyone turns on air-conditioners and "brownouts" are sometimes experienced.

OTHER FORMS OF SOLAR ENERGY

In addition to the effects of the Sun's direct rays, solar energy appears in other forms as well. Winds are driven by the Sun's heating effects, and winds and heating are responsible for the currents that flow in the oceans. Also, temperature differences (*thermal gradients*) exist between surface and deep waters because of solar heating. Energy has been extracted from winds for centuries through the use of windmills, and, at least in principle, it is possible to obtain useful amounts of power by harnessing ocean currents and by tapping thermal gradients. No real efforts have yet been made to test these latter possibilities.

In Denmark and Hungary, 0.2-MWe windmill generators have been successfully operated continuously for long periods. But these are huge, ungainly, and relatively inefficient devices. Recent advances in using strong, lightweight materials and sophisticated aerodynamic designs now make it possible to construct much more efficient and smaller generators. It appears likely that these new wind-driven generators will be used to provide power in many remote locations where the electrical network has not yet penetrated and where relatively small amounts of power are required. On the other hand, it seems unrealistic to suppose that a substantial fraction of our electrical power will ever be generated by the winds. Any scheme to utilize wind power on a large scale suffers from the obvious problem of visual pollution. Who would like to see, as one proposal has it, 15,000 generating towers, each 850 feet high and spaced 400 feet apart, extending from Texas to North Dakota?

ENERGY STORAGE

One of the problems associated with the generation of electricity is that the demand for power fluctuates. During the day the power requirements, especially for commercial purposes, are much greater than during the nighttime hours. If there were some way to *store*

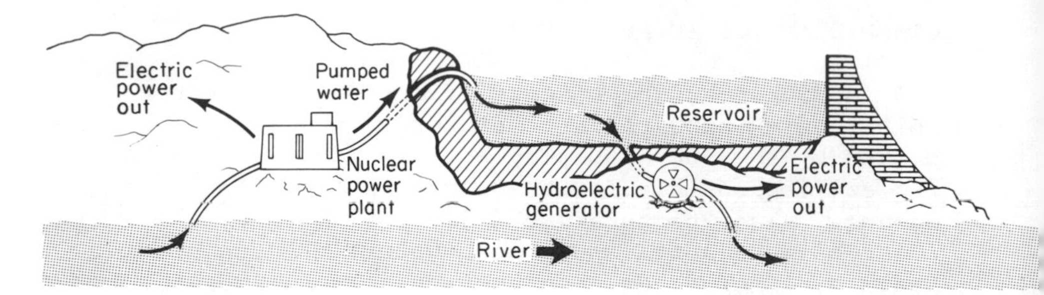

Figure 4.12 Schematic of a pumped storage system. Water is pumped into the reservoir during off-peak hours by electrical pumps powered by the output of the generator station. The water is later allowed to flow through a hydroelectric generator, producing electrical power at times of high demand.

electrical energy, the generating plants could be operated at capacity during the night, storing up energy to be released when the demand increases. But how can electrical energy be stored? For small-scale uses, we have *batteries*; however, for the large energy requirements of homes and industry, batteries are completely impractical. One solution seems to be the pumped storage of water. At night, when the demand for power is low, instead of decreasing the operating level of the plant, some of the output power is used to pump water from a river or lake into a storage reservoir at a high elevation (Fig. 4.12). This water represents stored energy which can be recovered by allowing the water to return to the original height, turning a turbine generator on the way. By pumping during the night and adding the hydroelectric power to the plant's output during the day, the generated power can be more closely matched to the demand.

Although this scheme appears quite feasible and sensible, the plan requires the construction of an enormous water reservoir on a hill or plateau that is located near a river or lake. One of the proposals to construct a pumped storage system (on the Hudson River) has been challenged because of the environmental damage that would result from the construction of the reservoir. The largest pumped storage facility now in operation is located at Luddington, Michigan, and is operated jointly by the Consumers Power Company and the Detroit Edison Company. This plant uses Lake Michigan as the lower reservoir; the upper reservoir is a manmade lake 1.5 km by 3 km. The maximum power output is 1900 MWe and the energy storage capacity is 15,000,000 kWh.

One of the more interesting recent ideas regarding energy storage on a longer time scale is the proposal to make widespread use of hydrogen gas as a fuel. Ever since the disastrous accident in 1937 when the hydrogen-filled airship Hindenburg was consumed by flames, hydrogen has been considered too dangerous for public use. During the intervening years, however, we have developed the techniques for handling hydrogen with safety. In the space program, for example, liquid hydrogen and liquid oxygen have long been used as the propellants in our most powerful rockets. The most serious problem associated with the introduction of hydrogen as a major fuel is probably one of public acceptance.

Hydrogen offers an attractive possibility for the storage of electrical energy. Most hydrogen in use today is produced by *electrolysis*—an electrical current is passed through water, and it dissociates into hydrogen and oxygen. The component elements can be recombined into water with the release of energy directly in the electrical form in devices called *fuel cells*, or the hydrogen gas can be burned and the heat used in the same way that the heat from the burning of natural gas is used.

By operating electrical generating plants at full capacity (which is the condition of maximum efficiency), electrical power could be supplied to meet the immediate requirements and any excess power could be used to electrolyze water into hydrogen and oxygen. Hydrogen, instead of electricity, could be delivered to homes and factories where it could be burned or where fuel cells could produce electricity on the spot as needed.

Hydrogen possesses a number of advantages as a fuel for space heating. Natural gas is the cleanest of the fossil fuels. When natural gas is burned, only carbon dioxide and water (and sometimes carbon monoxide) are produced. On the other hand, when hydrogen burns, *only* water is formed:

$$2\ H_2 + O_2 \longrightarrow 2\ H_2O$$

Hydrogen is therefore the cleanest possible combustible fuel. (An added benefit is that *pure* water is produced and could assist in meeting the local demand for water.)

The energy content of hydrogen gas is only about one-third of that of natural gas—about 95 kWh per 1000 ft^3 for hydrogen, compared to about 300 kWh per 1000 ft^3 for natural gas. But hydrogen burns with a hotter flame, and because no noxious fumes are produced, it can be burned in an unvented space. (A home furnace using hydrogen gas could perhaps be operated without a flue or chimney. There might be some problems arising from the production of nitrogen oxides in the heated air.) Hydrogen could be stored in central depots and routed to homes and factories through the underground pipeline system now used to deliver natural gas.

Is it possible to store solar energy? This is done, of course, in the formation of coal and oil, but these are long-term processes which cannot be speeded up. One of the ideas for the storing of solar energy is to allow solar radiation to promote the biochemical processes that convert our organic waste materials into useful chemical fuels (such as methane and hydrogen gas). This attractive idea is still in the development stage, but several pilot projects are under way. It appears unlikely that the fuels derived from wastes will ever amount to more than 1 or 2 percent of our national requirements, but at least there is the possibility that our wastes can be put to some good use.

Another way in which solar energy is stored is in the growth of plants such as food substances (which we use as fuel in our bodies) and trees (which we use hardly at all as fuel). In 1972 the domestic harvesting of wood amounted to 130×10^6 tons. Most of this wood is used as lumber or converted into paper products. If it were all burned, the thermal energy output would be about 0.4×10^{12} kWh. At a conversion efficiency of 40 percent, the annual wood crop could yield 0.16×10^{12} kWh of electrical energy, or about 10 percent of the amount used in the United States each year. Because of the large effect on our forest lands, it does not appear likely that we will attempt to double our wood harvest in order to supplement our electrical output by only 10 percent. (It should be noted, however, that wood contains very little sulfur so that one of the major problems associated with the burning of coal is not a factor in the use of wood as a fuel.) On the other hand, some electrical generating plants are being modified to use waste materials (primarily wood and paper trash) as fuels. In St. Louis a project is under way to utilize essentially all of the area's solid wastes in the generation of electricity. Scheduled for operation by mid-1977, the plant will be able to handle 2.5 to 3 million tons of solid wastes annually and to produce an average power of about 300 MWe. In addition to the production of useful amounts of power, the trash-burning system will help alleviate the trash disposal and land-fill problems.

A much more practical and efficient way to utilize forest products as fuel is to convert them to *methanol* (methyl or wood alcohol, CH_3OH). Methanol is a clean-burning, inexpensive, easily transported fuel. It can be used to supplement (and perhaps eventually even substitute for) our gasoline and other liquid fuel supplies. In fact, tests have shown that methanol mixed with gasoline in proportions up to 15 or 20 percent and used in standard automobile engines without modification will increase the performance (reduce acceleration time and improve mileage per gallon) and decrease the pollutants in the exhaust gases. Moreover, methanol can be produced from wood or coal or from almost any chemical fuel, and sold at prices below the current inflated prices for gasoline. It has been estimated that with proper management of our commercial forests, sufficient methanol could be produced to generate all of the electrical power that we now use. Because of the many attractive features of methanol, it would seem prudent and economical to begin shifting toward methanol as a primary liquid fuel.

QUESTIONS AND EXERCISES

1. Figure 4.1 shows that a much larger fraction of our energy needs were satisfied by coal in 1910 than today. Why has coal declined in use compared to other fuels?

2. By 1980, it will be possible to pump approximately 2×10^6 barrels of oil per day through the Trans-Alaska Pipeline from Prudhoe Bay on the Alaskan North Slope to the southern part of the state. (a) What fraction of the anticipated oil requirements in the United States in 1980 can be met by Alaskan oil? (b) The energy equivalent of one barrel of oil is 1700 kWh. What fraction of the U.S. energy requirements for 1980 could pass through this pipeline? (c) A barrel of oil has a mass of approximately 310 lb. How many 100,000-ton tanker loads would be required annually to transport the amount of oil carried by the proposed pipeline?

3. The *plant efficiency factor* of an electrical generating facility is defined to be the ratio of the actual amount of electrical energy delivered to the amount that could have been delivered if the plant had operated full time at maximum capacity. Usually, the factor is computed on the basis of a year's operation. (Shutdowns and operations at below peak capacity during low-load hours make the plant efficiency factor always less than 100%.) Compute the plant efficiency factor for all U.S. facilities taken together by considering that in 1971, the installed capacity was about 350,000 MWe and the delivered electrical energy amounted to 1.6×10^{12} kWh. Do you think your result is reasonable? Explain.

4. Assume that it would be possible to extract 0.1 percent of the deuterium in the ocean waters. How long would the fusion energy from this deuterium supply the world-wide needs at the present rate of energy consumption?

5. Suppose that it requires $2 billion to construct a 1000-MWe solar farm. The farm operates 8 hours a day at an average of 70 percent of peak capacity. How much of a surcharge (in cents per kWh) must be placed on the price charged the consumer if the capital cost of the plant is to be recovered in 30 years? Compare this with the present cost of electrical energy. What advantages do conventional and nuclear power plants have over solar farms with regard to the recovery of capital costs? How much difference does this make?

Chapter 5
NUCLEAR POWER

The survey of energy resources presented in the preceding chapter strongly suggests that we are facing a future in which nuclear power will play a major if not a dominant role. The reason is simple enough. Our supplies of fossil fuels are being depleted and we are forced to seek new sources of energy. At the present time, we do not know how to exploit solar energy or geothermal energy on a large scale nor do we know how to extract the petroleum locked in shale deposits in an economically feasible way. And we do not know how to obtain useful amounts of energy from nuclear fusion reactions.

Probably all of these technological problems will eventually be solved, perhaps even within a relatively short time. But we cannot be certain of this. We would be courting disaster if we planned our future under the assumption that fusion reactors or solar power plants would be operational by the year 2000 or even by the year 2025. The one new source of energy that we *know* how to exploit is nuclear fission energy. However, nuclear fission reactors produce huge amounts of radioactivity. Is the potential hazard of radioactivity accidentally released into the atmosphere or water supply so great that we should no longer permit the proliferation of nuclear power plants? Can we afford to forego the use of fission energy in the vague hope that some breakthrough will suddenly provide us with cheap, clean energy? Or is it more reasonable to hedge our bets by proceeding with the development of nuclear power while continuing and increasing our efforts to discover feasible ways to exploit alternate sources of energy?

The answers to these questions constitute the key to the energy picture for the next several decades, perhaps for a hundred years. Therefore, we devote this chapter to a discussion of the nuclear fission and fusion processes and to some details of nuclear reactor operations. In the next chapter we concentrate on the problem of radioactivity and its effects on Man, both bad and good.

PROTONS, NEUTRONS, AND NUCLEI

Before we proceed with our main discussion, let us review some of the basic facts about nuclei. Every atom has at its core a tiny nucleus which contains most of the mass of the atom. The size of a nucleus is extremely small compared to the size of an atom. The diameter of an atom is typically 10^{-10} m, whereas nuclear diameters are about 10^{-14} m, or about 10,000 times smaller.

Nuclei consist of protons and neutrons. The nucleus of the normal hydrogen atom is a single proton, but all other nuclei consist of both protons (which carry positive electrical charge) and neutrons (which are electrically neutral). A nucleus which contains a total of A protons and neutrons is said to have a *mass number* equal to A. The element hydrogen occurs in three forms with different nuclear mass numbers (Fig. 5.1):

^{1}H: $A = 1$ (1 proton). This is the most abundant form of hydrogen; 99.985 percent of all hydrogen in Nature is ^{1}H.

^{2}H: $A = 2$ (1 proton plus 1 neutron). This is heavy hydrogen (or *deuterium*); the natural abundance of ^{2}H is 0.015 percent.

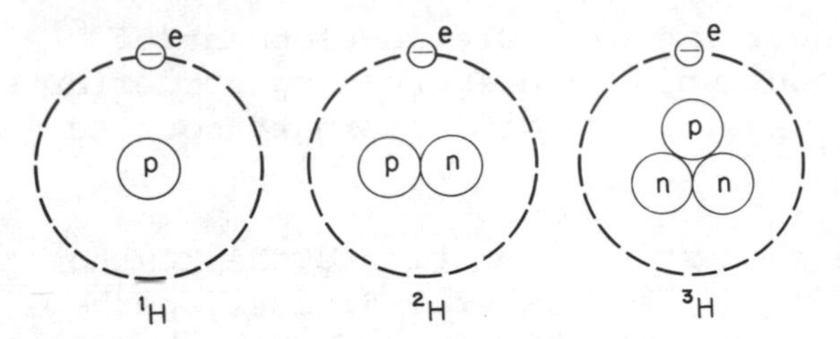

Figure 5.1 The three isotopes of hydrogen. In each case the nucleus contains one proton, but the number of neutrons in each isotope is different.

^{3}H: A = 3 (1 proton plus 2 neutrons). This form of hydrogen (called *tritium*) is radioactive; it does not occur naturally and must be produced by artificial means (by nuclear reactions).

The different nuclear forms of a particular element are called *isotopes*. Thus, there are three different isotopes of hydrogen: ^{1}H, ^{2}H, and ^{3}H. (No isotope of hydrogen exists with a mass number greater than 3.) All uranium nuclei contain 92 protons; the important isotopes of uranium contain 143 neutrons (^{235}U) and 146 neutrons (^{238}U). Notice that the mass number of an isotope is always given as a left-hand superscript to the element symbol.

The number of protons in a nucleus (or the number of electrons in the normal atom) is called the *atomic number* of the element and is indicated by the letter Z. Thus hydrogen has Z = 1 and uranium has Z = 92.

NUCLEAR MASSES

The masses of nuclei are measured on a scale in which the mass of the atom of the most abundant isotope of carbon (^{12}C, 6 protons plus 6 neutrons) is exactly 12. Thus we say that the mass of ^{12}C is 12 *atomic mass units* or 12 AMU. In metric units,

$$1 \text{ AMU} = 1.66 \times 10^{-27} \text{ kg} \qquad (5.1)$$

The masses of the proton and the neutron on this scale are approximately but not exactly equal to 1:

$$\left.\begin{aligned} m_{\text{proton}} &= 1.0073 \text{ AMU} \\ m_{\text{neutron}} &= 1.0087 \text{ AMU} \end{aligned}\right\} \qquad (5.2)$$

The mass of a nucleus does not exactly equal the sum of the masses of the constituent protons and neutrons. There is always a small but extremely important difference. For example, consider the nucleus of deuterium (^{2}H) which consists of one proton and one neutron. The mass of the deuterium nucleus is 2.0136 AMU. Comparing with the sum of the masses given in Eq. 5.1, we find

$$\begin{aligned} m_{\text{proton}} + m_{\text{neutron}} &= 2.0160 \text{ AMU} \\ m_{\text{deuterium}} &= 2.0136 \text{ AMU} \\ \hline \text{Difference} &= 0.0024 \text{ AMU} \end{aligned}$$

That is, the mass of the deuterium nucleus is *smaller* by 0.0024 AMU than the combined mass of a proton and a neutron.

What is the significance of this mass difference? One of the results derived by Einstein from his theory of relativity is that a *mass* difference is entirely equivalent to an *energy* difference. The equation which expresses this relationship is the famous Einstein mass-energy equation,

$$E = mc^2 \qquad (5.3)$$

where c is the speed of light. This equation states that if the mass of a system is changed by an amount m, the energy of that system is changed by an amount mc^2. If we use $c = 3 \times 10^8$ m/s and the value of 1 AMU expressed in kilograms (Eq. 5.1), we can easily compute

$$(1 \text{ AMU}) \times c^2 = 4.98 \times 10^{-17} \text{ J} \qquad (5.4)$$

Because nuclear energies are so small when expressed in joules, we usually employ a different unit called the *electron volt* (eV). One electron volt is the kinetic energy acquired by a proton (or an electron) when it is accelerated through a potential difference of one volt. In terms of joules,

$$1 \text{ eV} = 1.60 \times 10^{-19} \text{ J} \tag{5.5}$$

Larger units are

$$\begin{aligned} 1 \text{ kiloelectron volt} &= 1 \text{ keV} = 10^{3} \text{ eV} = 1.60 \times 10^{-16} \text{ J} \\ 1 \text{ megaelectron volt} &= 1 \text{ MeV} = 10^{6} \text{ eV} = 1.60 \times 10^{-13} \text{ J} \end{aligned} \tag{5.6}$$

Equation 5.4 can therefore be written as

$$(1 \text{ AMU}) \times c^2 = 931 \text{ MeV} \tag{5.7}$$

In these terms, the mass difference found for deuterium (0.0024 AMU) amounts to an energy difference of 2.2 MeV.

What does an *energy* difference mean in this case? Our system consists of one proton and one neutron, and we can imagine changing between a condition in which the particles are free from one another and another condition in which the particles are bound together as a deuterium nucleus. If we wish to convert a deuterium nucleus into a free proton and a free neutron, we must *increase* the mass of the system. That is, we must supply energy to a deuterium nucleus in order to split it into its component parts. If this amount of energy (or more) is not supplied, the deuterium nucleus can never break apart—it is *bound* by 2.2 MeV, and this energy value is called the *binding energy* of the nucleus. The *smaller* the mass of a nucleus (compared to the mass of the same number of free protons and neutrons), the *greater* is the binding energy of the nucleus.

All nuclei have this property possessed by the deuterium nucleus. *All* nuclei have masses that are smaller than the combined masses of the constituent protons and neutrons

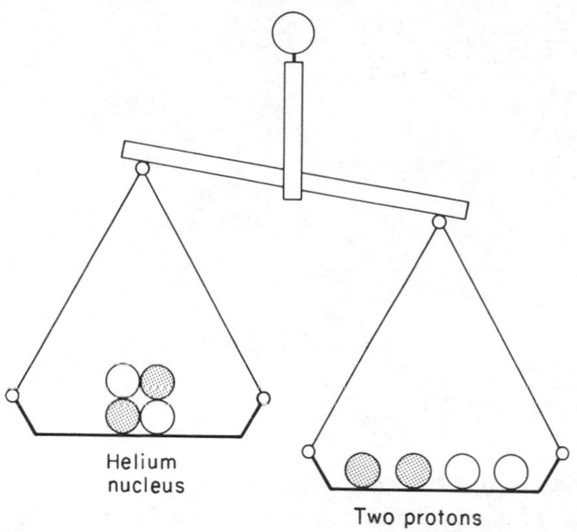

Figure 5.2 The mass of any nucleus (for example, the helium nucleus shown here) is smaller *than the combined mass of the constituent protons and neutrons in the free state. The mass difference corresponds to the* binding energy *of the nucleus.*

(Fig. 5.2). Indeed, independent and precise measurements of nuclear masses and binding energies have been used to verify the correctness of the Einstein mass-energy relation.

THE BINDING ENERGY CURVE

One of the most useful ways to summarize the information that has been accumulated regarding nuclear masses is to plot the data in the way shown in Fig. 5.3. The binding energy of deuterium is 2.2 MeV, but the binding energy of ^{235}U is 1760 MeV. Therefore, in order to show the vast range of binding energies on a convenient scale, we divide the binding energy of a nucleus by its mass number A. That is, the quantity plotted is the binding energy *per particle* in the nucleus. As seen in Fig. 5.3 this quantity is approximately the same for most nuclei, varying

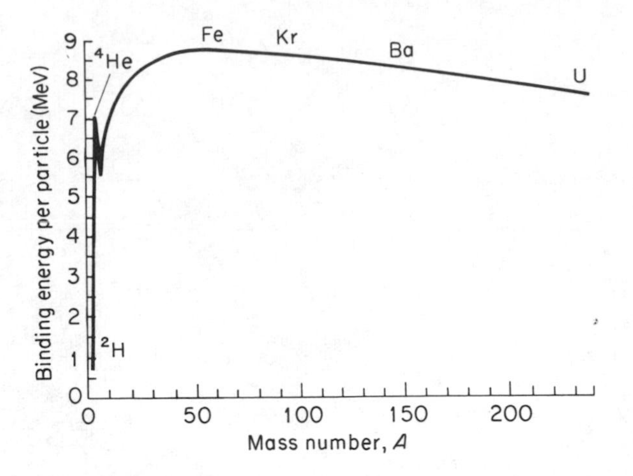

Figure 5.3 The nuclear binding energy curve. The binding energy per particle in the nucleus reaches a maximum in the vicinity of iron and gradually decreases toward heavier elements.

only between 7.5 and 8.7 MeV per particle for all A greater than about 16. The lighter nuclei have somewhat smaller binding energies.

The binding energy curve reaches a maximum for nuclei in the vicinity of iron (Fe) and then gradually decreases toward the heavier elements. This behavior is responsible for the fact that the *fusion* and *fission* processes release energy.

NUCLEAR FISSION

In 1938, just before the outbreak of the second world war in Europe, the German radiochemists Otto Hahn and Fritz Strassman bombarded uranium with neutrons and studied the radioactive material that resulted from the interaction. Hahn and Strassman found that the products of the uranium-plus-neutron reaction included radioactive barium ($Z = 56$), an element with a mass much less than that of the original uranium ($Z = 92$). What kind of reaction could produce a nucleus so much lighter than the bombarded nucleus? The mystery was soon solved by Lise Meitner and Otto Frisch, refugees from Nazi Germany, who were then working in Sweden. Meitner and Frisch suggested that the absorption of neutrons by uranium produced a breakup (or *fission*) of the nucleus into two fragments, each with a mass roughly one-half the mass of the original uranium nucleus:

$$U(Z = 92) + n \longrightarrow Ba(Z = 56) + Kr(Z = 36) \qquad (5.8)$$

It was promptly recognized that the fission process offered the possibility for the release of nuclear energy on a gigantic scale.

The graph in Fig. 5.3 shows that the binding energy of uranium is approximately 7.5 MeV per particle, whereas the binding energies for barium and krypton are each about 8.5 MeV per particle. That is, the combined mass of barium and krypton is approximately 1 MeV per particle *less* than the mass of uranium. Thus, when a uranium nucleus splits into nuclei of barium and krypton, there is an energy release of about 1 MeV for each proton and neutron involved. The fission of each uranium nucleus therefore releases just over 200 MeV of energy.

Because the binding energy curve exhibits a smooth decrease from iron to uranium, there is nothing unique about the particular fission process, U + n ⟶ Ba + Kr. Essentially the same amount of energy would be released in the fission of uranium into two other nuclei, for example,

$$U(Z = 92) + n \longrightarrow Ce(Z = 58) + Se(Z = 34) \qquad (5.9a)$$

or,

$$U(Z = 92) + n \longrightarrow Xe(Z = 54) + Sr(Z = 38) \qquad (5.9b)$$

Indeed, both of these fission processes, as well as many others, have been observed. Moreover, any heavy nucleus can undergo fission and many have been studied, but only two—uranium and plutonium—have been utilized in large-scale applications.

© 1933 NY Herald Tribune Co

SEPTEMBER 12, 1933

Lord Rutherford

Atom-Powered World Absurd, Scientists Told

Lord Rutherford Scoffs at Theory of Harnessing Energy in Laboratories

By The Associated Press

LEICESTER, England, Sept. 11.—Lord Rutherford, at whose Cambridge laboratories atoms have been bombarded and split into fragments, told an audience of scientists today that the idea of releasing tremendous power from within the atom was absurd.

He addressed the British Association for the Advancement of Science in the same hall where the late Lord Kelvin asserted twenty-six years ago that the atom was indestructible.

Describing the shattering of atoms by use of 5,000,000 volts of electricity, Lord Rutherford discounted hopes advanced by some scientists that profitable power could be thus extracted.

"The energy produced by the breaking down of the atom is a very poor kind of thing," he said. "Any one who expects a source of power from the transformation of these atoms is talking moonshine. . . . We hope in the next few years to get some idea of what these atoms are, how they are made and the way they are worked."

Figure 5.4 Ernest Rutherford won a Nobel Prize for his studies of radioactivity and he pioneered the investigation of nuclear reactions. His keen insight had enabled him to make enormous progress in unraveling the mysteries of the nucleus, but his prophecy concerning the future of atomic power proved to be completely in error. The views expressed more than a decade earlier by the British scientist, Sir Oliver Lodge, were more accurate. In 1920, Lodge wrote, "The time will come when atomic energy will take the place of coal as a source of power... I hope that the human race will not discover how to use this energy until it has brains enough to use it properly...".

An energy release of 200 MeV per nucleus represents a staggering amount of energy that is available in a bulk sample of a heavy element. The fission energy that can be released from 1 kg of uranium is sufficient to raise the temperature of 200,000,000 gallons of water from room temperature to the boiling point (approximately 23 million kWh).

CHAIN REACTIONS

When a heavy nucleus undergoes fission, not only are two lighter nuclear fragments formed, but two or three neutrons are released as well. Therefore, Eq. 5.8 expressed in more detail is

$$^{235}U + n \rightarrow {}^{139}Ba + {}^{94}Kr + 3n \quad (5.10a)$$

or,

$$^{235}U + n \rightarrow {}^{139}Ba + {}^{95}Kr + 2n \quad (5.10b)$$

Most of the isotopes produced in fission processes (for example, ^{139}Ba, ^{94}Kr, ^{95}Kr, as well as many others) are *highly radioactive*.

The fact that a fission event is induced by *one* neutron and the event releases *two* or *three* neutrons means that it is possible to construct a system in which the fission process is *self-sustaining*. If each of the neutrons released in a primary fission event is absorbed by another uranium nucleus producing additional events, the process multiplies rapidly and can consume all of the available uranium in a small fraction of a second. Figure 5.5 shows schematically the cascading of fission events (a *chain reaction*) that leads to the rapid release of the fission energy—a nuclear explosion. This is the principle of the *atomic bomb* (properly, a *nuclear* bomb).

In order for a fission device to explode, the cascading of the fission events is essential—the neutrons must be prevented from leaving the sample so that they are available

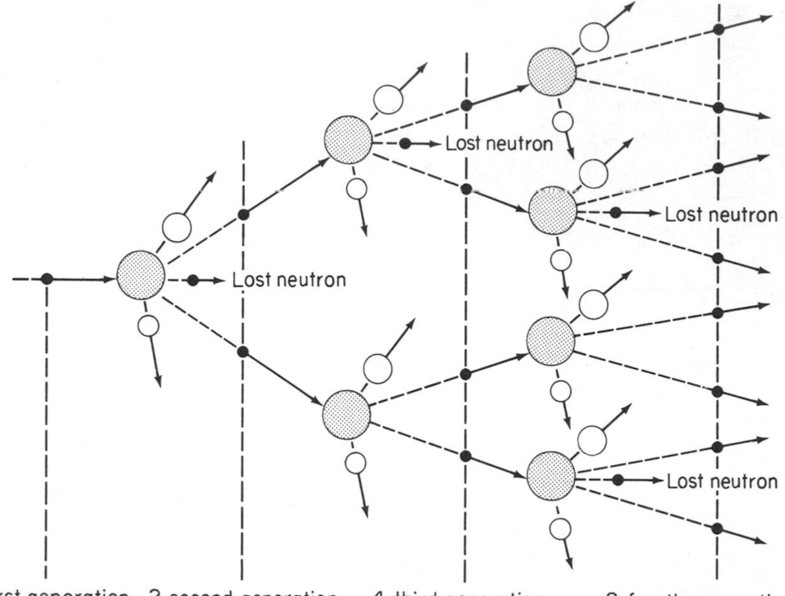

Figure 5.5 An uncontrolled chain reaction of fission events. Each event releases two or three neutrons; in each case two neutrons are shown initiating new fission events and the third neutron (if released) is assumed to leave the sample. The uncontrolled multiplication of fission events leads to a nuclear explosion.

to induce additional fission events. If the sample is too small, neutrons will escape and an insufficient number of fission events will take place in a short time to constitute an explosion. (The sample will merely become hot.) But if the sample is large enough, the neutrons will be contained and an explosion will result. The minimum size is called the *critical mass* of the material. One of the major problems in constructing a nuclear bomb is to devise a method for bringing together two subcritical masses (which cannot explode) into a single mass that is greater than the critical mass (and which will immediately explode). This problem was solved by the scientists and engineers of the Manhattan Project in 1945. The details are still classified information but it is known that the critical mass of ^{235}U is several kilograms.

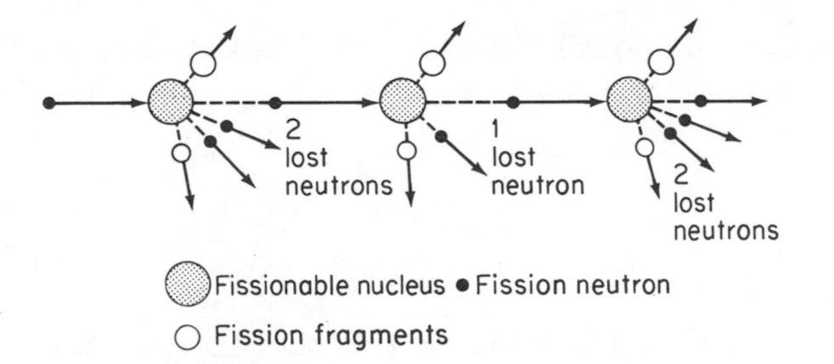

Figure 5.6 The rate at which energy is released from nuclear fission can be controlled by arranging a system in which exactly one neutron from each fission event initiates another event. In this way, the cascading process characteristic of an explosive device (Fig. 5.5) is avoided.

The first explosive atomic device was detonated on July 16, 1945, in the desert near Alamagordo, New Mexico. The device had been prepared by a huge scientific team from the Allied countries working in the Manhattan Project laboratory at Los Alamos, New Mexico. After the successful Alamagordo test, two weapons of different design were constructed and made available to the military. These weapons were dropped on the Japanese cities of Hiroshima and Nagasaki in August 1945. The explosions caused more than 100,000 casualties and forced the Imperial Japanese government to capitulate, thus ending World War II.

If the fission events in a sample of uranium are allowed to multiply in an uncontrolled way, an explosion results. But if the system is designed so that, on the average, exactly *one* neutron from each fission event triggers another event (Fig. 5.6), the fission energy can be released in a slow and controlled manner. This is the basic operating principle of the nuclear *reactor*. The construction and operation of reactors are discussed in the following section.

A self-sustaining chain reaction is analogous to population growth. An uncontrolled chain reaction, in which the number of neutrons continues to grow, corresponds to "population explosion." A controlled chain reaction, in which the number of neutrons remains constant, corresponds to "zero population growth."

PLUTONIUM

Naturally occurring uranium consists of the isotopes ^{238}U (99.3 percent) and ^{235}U (0.7 percent). The isotope which undergoes fission when it absorbs a slowly moving neutron is ^{235}U. When ^{238}U absorbs a slow neutron, ^{239}U is formed and fission does not take place. Consequently, natural uranium cannot be used in a conventional chain-reacting device because the abundant isotope ^{238}U absorbs too many neutrons for the reaction to be self-sustaining. One of the major problems faced by the Manhattan Project scientists was to devise a method to separate ^{235}U from natural uranium so that the fissioning isotope would be free from the difficulties produced by its isotopic partner. The separation techniques developed during the war years are still used to process the large quantities of uranium required by the nuclear power industry.

The isotope ^{238}U, although it does not undergo fission in the presence of slow neutrons, is nevertheless useful in preparing fission fuel. When ^{238}U absorbs a neutron, it becomes ^{239}U, a radioactive isotope. The β decay of ^{239}U produces the element *neptunium* (Np, $Z = 93$):

$$^{239}U \xrightarrow{\beta \text{ decay}} {}^{239}Np \quad (^{239}U \text{ half-life} = 23.5 \text{ min})$$

The new isotope ^{239}Np is also radioactive and decays to *plutonium* (Pu, $Z = 94$):

$$^{239}Np \xrightarrow{\beta \text{ decay}} {}^{239}Pu \quad (^{239}Np \text{ half-life} = 2.35 \text{ days})$$

^{239}Pu is also radioactive, but the half-life for decay is sufficiently long (24,360 years) that substantial quantities of the isotope can be accumulated. The importance of ^{239}Pu lies in the fact that it undergoes fission as readily as does ^{235}U. Therefore, ^{238}U can be converted into a useful fission fuel. Many of the fission devices now available, including certain types of reactors and various military weapons, utilize plutonium as the fission material. As we will see later in this chapter, the conversion of ^{238}U into the nuclear fuel ^{239}Pu and the similar conversion of ^{232}Th into ^{233}U are basic to the operation of *breeder reactors*.

ISOTOPIC ENRICHMENT OF URANIUM

Because ^{235}U represents only a small fraction of natural uranium, enrichment procedures must be carried out on uranium extracted from ores in order to increase the percentage of ^{235}U in a sample intended for use as a reactor fuel. (Some types of reactors operate with natural uranium or with minimal enrichments of ^{235}U; however, these reactors have not yet been demonstrated to be economically feasible as commercial power reactors.) Depending on the type of reactor in which the uranium will be used, the enrichment process must raise the fraction of ^{235}U from 0.7 percent to between 2 and 90 percent. Most of the uranium enriched in this country is processed in gaseous diffusion plants, the first of which was constructed at Oak Ridge, Tennessee during World War II. The principle of operation depends on the fact that a gas molecule (uranium hexafluoride, UF_6) containing the light isotope ^{235}U will diffuse through a porous barrier slightly more rapidly than one containing the heavy isotope ^{238}U. Enrichment plants of this type are expensive to construct and consume huge amounts of power when operated at peak capacity. In fact, the peak power requirement of the U.S. enrichment plants represents almost one-quarter of the total electrical power now generated by nuclear reactors in this country! The enrichment process is not nearly as inefficient as it seems from this figure, however, because some of the output is for foreign reactors, some is for military weapons (which require high enrichment and therefore large energy expenditures), and some is added to our stockpiles.

The enrichment of uranium represents a substantial part of the cost of preparing fuel for reactors. Consequently, considerable efforts have recently been made to develop alternate and more efficient methods of enrichment. Ultracentrifuge techniques are being used in which a sample is swung at high speeds, thus forcing the heavier isotope toward the outside of the apparatus. A new method using lasers is also being tried. The operating principle is based on the fact that the electron structure of an atom of ^{235}U is slightly different from that of an atom of ^{238}U. A laser is precisely tuned so that the light will excite the electrons of a ^{235}U atom but not those of a ^{238}U atom. The light from a second laser will then ionize the ^{235}U atoms but not the ^{238}U atoms. An electric field will therefore cause the ^{235}U ions to be removed from the sample and they can be collected on a plate while the ^{238}U atoms remain behind. Techniques such as the centrifuge method (or perhaps the laser method) may substantially reduce the enrichment costs in the future.

NUCLEAR REACTORS

When a heavy nucleus undergoes fission, most of the 200 MeV of energy that is released appears in the form of kinetic energy of the fission fragments. The rapidly moving fragments collide with the atoms in the sample and quickly dissipate their energy. As a result, the energy that represents the mass difference between the heavy nucleus and the fission fragments eventually appears as *heat*.

In the generation of electrical power from fossil fuels, chemical energy is extracted by burning the fuels in order to heat water and convert it into steam. The steam is then used to turn a turbine which operates an electrical generator. Many of the nuclear power plants in operation today are similar in design. The main difference is that a fission reactor is used to produce the high-pressure steam; the subsequent steps in generating electricity are the same as those in a conventional power plant.

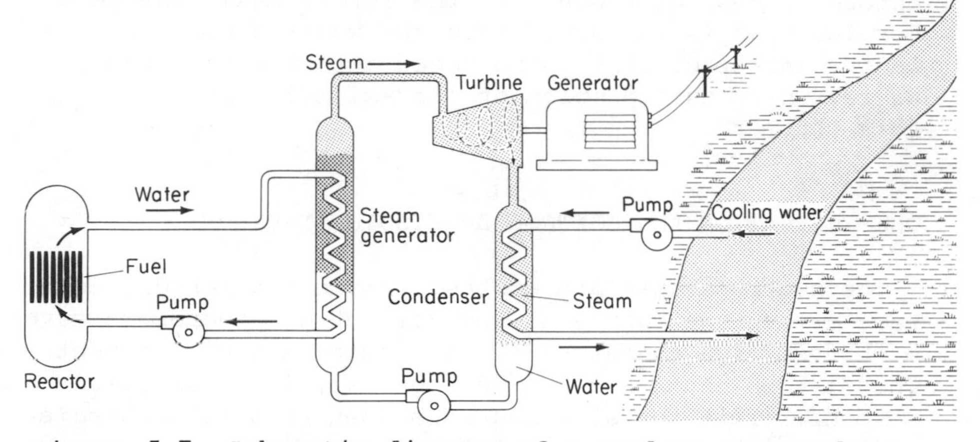

Figure 5.7 Schematic diagram of a nuclear power plant. The water in the loop that passes through the core of the reactor is at high pressure. This type of system is called a pressurized water reactor *(PWR). Here, the cooling water is shown being drawn from a river, but many of the newer plants use cooling towers so that excess heat is exhausted into the atmosphere instead of bodies of water. Some reactor designs use a gas such as carbon dioxide or helium as the coolant. These systems offer a slightly higher efficiency in the transfer of heat from the core to the steam generator.*

A schematic diagram of a pressurized water reactor is shown in Fig. 5.7. Water is pumped through the core of the reactor which is at a temperature of about 1200°C. High-pressure water emerges at a temperature of 300°C and converts the water in a second loop into steam. This steam passes into a turbine where it turns the blades at high speeds. The turbine shaft is connected to an electrical generator which produces electrical power that is fed into the power network over conventional transmission lines.

Figure 5.7 also shows that the steam exhausted from the turbine (now at a lower temperature) is condensed back to water by cooling coils supplied with water from some sort of reservoir. The source of this cooling water can be a river or bay, or it can be water that is circulated through a cooling tower. In the former case, the reactor's surplus heat is exhausted into the water system, whereas in the latter case it is released into the atmosphere. We return to this problem of *thermal pollution* later in this chapter.

THE MODERATION AND CONTROL OF FISSION NEUTRONS

The neutrons that are emitted in the fission process have an average energy of several MeV and therefore move with very high speeds. Fission neutrons are *fast* neutrons. The fission of ^{235}U or ^{239}Pu, however, is considerably more efficient for *slow* neutrons (neutrons with energies of 1 eV or less) than for fast neutrons. Consequently, the design of an efficient reactor must include a provision for slowing down (or *moderating*) the fast fission neutrons.

If a billiard ball makes a head-on collision with an identical stationary ball, the laws of energy and momentum conservation demand that the moving ball stop and that the struck ball move off with the same velocity as the original incoming ball. On the other hand, if the billiard ball strikes a bowling ball, the billiard ball will be deflected and only a small amount of energy will be transferred to the bowling ball. The same principles hold when a neutron collides with the nucleus of an atom. In the head-on collision between a neutron and a stationary proton (which has a mass essentially equal to that of the neutron), the proton is set into motion and the neutron comes to rest. Because the proton (unlike the neutron) is a *charged* particle, it rapidly loses its energy through electrical interactions with atomic electrons. Even if the collision is not exactly head-on, a substantial fraction of the neutron's kinetic energy will be transferred to the proton. If the struck nucleus is more massive than the neutron, a smaller amount of energy will be transferred and a large number of collisions will be necessary to slow the neutron from the MeV energy range to an energy near 1 eV.

The most effective neutron moderator is *hydrogen,* the only material whose nuclear mass is equal to that of the neutron. However, hydrogen has a drawback as a moderator—instead of always deflecting a neutron and carrying off some of its kinetic energy, hydrogen will sometimes *capture* a neutron, forming deuterium (^2H), thereby preventing the neutron from inducing a fission event. One solution is to use as a moderator *heavy water* in which deuterium is substituted for hydrogen in the water molecules. Deuterium has a low probability for capturing neutrons and the mass is sufficiently small to be an effective moderator. Heavy water, however, is expensive to produce and only a few reactors use this substance as a moderator. The most common practice is to accept the losses associated with neutron capture in water and to use normal (or *light*) water as a moderator and as a coolant.

In addition to a moderator that slows down the fast fission neutrons, a reactor must be provided with a means for controlling the number of neutrons available to induce fission events so that each event contributes, on the average, exactly one neutron that triggers a new event. This function is performed by a material, such as boron, which has a high probability of capturing slow neutrons. By moving *control rods* (usually made from boron carbide) into or out of the reactor core, the number of effective neutrons per fission event can be maintained at the desired value. Furthermore, by dropping into the core several control rods, the chain reaction can be quickly stopped in the event that the reactor must be shut down for maintenance or in an emergency.

The central part of a reactor therefore consists of four main components: uranium (or, in special types of reactors, plutonium) fuel, a moderator, control rods, and the heat transfer coils that carry water or some other coolant (see Fig. 5.8). The uranium fuel is in the form of long cylinders that are clad with a strong metal jacket. The fuel rods must be able to withstand the high temperatures at which all reactors operate. The fragments that result from the fission process are always highly radioactive. Therefore, another requirement on

Figure 5.8 The reactor vessel head is being lowered over the control rod drive shafts after the core was first fully loaded with fuel assemblies. This Point Beach nuclear plant at Two Creeks, Wisconsin is a pressurized water nuclear reactor which started operation in 1970. [Courtesy of Wisconsin Electric Power Co.]

the cladding of fuel rods is that it not leak its radioactive contents into the reactor during operation nor into the environment when removed for replacement.

THE NUCLEAR POWER INDUSTRY

In 1957 the Duquesne Light Company began operating the world's first commercial power-producing nuclear reactor. This unit, located at Shippingport, Pennsylvania, produces 90 MWe of electrical power. By present standards, Shippingport Unit 1 is a small power station. Most of the nuclear power plants recently opened or under construction have power ratings in the vicinity of 1000 MWe (Fig. 5.9).

Figure 5.9 The San Onofre nuclear generating station near San Clemente, California has an electrical capacity of 430 MWe and began operation in 1967. [Courtesy of Southern California Edison Co.]

At the end of 1971, there were 21 stations operating in the United States, with a total capacity of 8400 MWe. By 1973 the number had risen to 42 stations with a total capacity of 25,670 MWe. This latter figure represents 5.6 percent of the present total electrical generating capacity of the United States (460,000 MWe). More than 50 plants are under construction and over 100 are under firm order. It is anticipated that the fraction of the total electrical generating capacity contributed by nuclear power plants will be 12 percent in 1975, 21 percent in 1980, and 33 percent in 1985. By the year 2000, the Atomic Energy Commission expects that nuclear energy will account for the majority of the electrical power produced in this country.

The construction of nuclear power facilities is expensive. At present, the real cost (including interest on capital during construction) is approximately $500 per installed kilowatt. Thus, a modern 1000-MWe nuclear power

TABLE 5.1
Significant Events in the Development of Nuclear Power

1939	Discovery of nuclear fission
1940	Discovery of plutonium
1942	First self-sustaining fission chain reaction
1945	First successful test of an explosive fission device; first (and only) use of nuclear weapons in warfare
1946	U.S. Atomic Energy Commission established
1951	First significant amount of electric power (100 kWe) produced from a test reactor
1954	Commissioning of first nuclear-powered submarine, Nautilus
1957	First reactor designed exclusively for the production of commercial electric power becomes operational (Shippingport, Pennsylvania)
1972	First breeder reactor becomes operational (U.S.S.R.)

plant costs about $500 million. By 1980 the investment in nuclear power facilities is expected to amount to $60 billion. Conventional coal- or oil-fired plants are somewhat less expensive. But it is difficult to make a direct comparison. The nuclear figure includes all of the costs required to meet the safety and environmental standards, whereas these costs are often not included in the quoted figures for conventional plants. However, a safe estimate is that a nuclear power plant costs about one and a half times as much as a conventional power plant per installed kilowatt.

Although the construction costs for a nuclear power plant are somewhat greater than for a coal-fired (or oil-fired) plant, the annual operating expenses are less. This is due primarily to the smaller cost for nuclear fuel compared to fossil fuel. A 1000-MWe coal-fired plant will require about $35 million of coal in a 1-year period, whereas a nuclear power plant of the same size uses only about $12 million of uranium each year. The net result is that nuclear power plants are competitive with coal-fired facilities in the generation of electricity. The greater efficiency of breeder reactors (when they become operational) will probably result in the production of electrical power at rates below that possible from conventional systems. Of course, the cost of electricity from either type of plant will be considerably higher at that time (probably about 1990) than it is now.

BREEDER REACTORS

The only naturally occurring isotope that undergoes fission with slow (moderated) neutrons is ^{235}U. Because ^{235}U constitutes only a small fraction (0.7 percent) of natural uranium, enormous quantities of uranium ore must be processed in order to provide fuel for slow-neutron reactors. The supplies of uranium ores are not unlimited. If we continue to use ^{235}U in the nuclear power plants that are projected until the year 2000, we will have exhausted all of the known reserves of high-quality ores and will then be using low-grade ores. The cost of extracting uranium from the ores will therefore increase and electrical energy will be more expensive.

We know that the abundant uranium isotope ^{238}U can be converted into ^{239}Pu which is an excellent fuel in slow-neutron reactors. Furthermore, thorium is a plentiful element and its single stable isotope ^{232}Th can be converted into ^{233}U by a neutron capture reaction followed by a β decay, a process analogous to the $^{238}U \longrightarrow {}^{239}Pu$ conversion. ^{233}U is radioactive but the half-life is long (162,000 years) so that bulk quantities of the isotope can be accumulated. ^{233}U is similar to ^{239}Pu in that it undergoes slow-neutron fission and can be used as a nuclear fuel.

Can we produce sufficient quantities of ^{239}Pu and ^{233}U to supply the increasing number of reactors with relatively inexpensive fuel? In any type of reactor, one neutron from each fission is required simply to maintain the chain reaction by inducing a new fission event. If one additional neutron is captured by ^{238}U or ^{232}Th, the fuel supply will remain constant—just as many fuel nuclei are produced as are used. A reactor which produces *more* fuel nuclei than it consumes is called a *breeder reactor*. These reactors, which have not yet been perfected to the degree of the present slow-neutron reactors, appear to offer the best hope for continued cheap electrical power during the unknown time interval before fusion reactors become operational. A breeder reactor will not only produce fuel to compensate for its own consumption, but it will also provide fuel for new reactors.

Experimental breeder reactors have been in operation in the United States and elsewhere for a number of years. But the first breeder reactor to produce commercially useful quantities of electrical power was a Soviet unit. This reactor, on the eastern shore of the Caspian Sea, began operating in early 1972 and produces 350 MWe of electrical power.

There are two types of breeder reactor systems. The slow-neutron breeder operates best on the ^{232}Th-^{233}U cycle. The so-called *fast* breeder operates without a moderator because the ^{238}U-^{239}Pu cycle is more efficient using unmoderated neutrons. In a fast breeder the nonproductive absorption of neutrons is less, and this increases the rate at which new fuel is produced. Most of the breeder systems now being studied are *fast* breeders.

Because there is no moderation of neutrons in a fast breeder, the cores of these reactors are quite small and the power density is much higher compared to that in slow-neutron reactors: The rate of production of heat in a breeder reactor will be about twice as great as in a slow-neutron reactor. At the higher temperatures and power densities in the cores of breeder reactors, water is no longer an effective way to remove heat from the core and transfer it to an exterior steam generator. Moreover, water would act as a moderator and this is undesirable in a fast breeder reactor. Therefore, instead of water, a liquid metal (such as sodium) is used in fast breeder reactors and they are called *liquid metal fast breeder reactors* (LMFBR).

LMFBRs have some special problems not shared by slow-neutron reactors. The control is much more delicate and extra considerations must be given to ensuring that the power level is maintained within safe operating limits. Sodium metal is chemically highly reactive and it must be carefully isolated from water and air. Furthermore, sodium becomes highly radioactive from neutron capture reactions as it passes through the reactor core. Therefore, extreme precautions must be taken to ensure the integrity of the intricate plumbing that pumps sodium through the core at a rate of more than 10,000 m^3/hr. Other designs for breeder reactors include those in which molten salt or a gas is used as the heat transfer medium. Some of the problems of LMFBRs do not arise in such reactors, but they have their own special technical difficulties. A substantial amount of additional development is required before breeder reactors can be placed into commercial service. In 1972, the United States announced a stepped-up program to make commercially viable breeder reactors a reality by the mid-1980s.

Breeder reactors have several advantages over the current generation of reactors. Low-grade ores can be used and the ^{238}U component can be converted into ^{239}Pu fuel. Moreover, the thermal efficiency will be comparable to that of fossil fuel power plants (40 percent). There seems to be no question that breeder reactors will be required eventually on a large scale if fission is to continue to be an economic means of generating electrical power.

BENEFIT VERSUS RISK

Our world today has expanding energy needs, a dwindling supply of fossil fuels, and an increasing awareness of the environmental aspects of energy production. Nuclear reactors offer the prospect of long-term relatively inexpensive power. Moreover, nuclear reactors generate electrical power without the smoke and fumes that are characteristic of fossil fuels and which have acknowledged adverse biological effects. Also, the mining of uranium produces much less degradation of the countryside than the mining of fossil fuels, particularly coal. But reactors have their own peculiar set of disadvantages, mainly associated with the production of radioactivity. We can divide the problems into several categories:

1. *Explosions and Meltdowns*. The interior of an operating reactor is always radioactively "hot" because fission reactions produce radioactive fragments and because neutrons produce radioactive isotopes when they are captured by most reactor construction materials. One of the fears that has been expressed concerning reactors is that in the event of some sort of accident, radioactive material could be strewn about the surrounding countryside with catastrophic consequences. The likelihood of the occurrence of such a disaster is extremely small. The construction of a reactor is entirely different from that of a nuclear weapon, so that an uncontrolled chain reaction leading to the weapon-like explosion of a reactor is not possible.

There does exist the remote possibility of a failure of the cooling system which could result in the *meltdown* of the reactor core. Every reactor is equipped with a backup cooling system and so the probability that a meltdown will ever occur is very small. But if a situation ever developed in which both cooling systems failed, the sudden temperature increase in the core would melt the structure before the automatic shutdown procedure could take effect. In such an accident the fuel rods would probably rupture and highly radioactive material would be released. But to forestall the possible spread of the dangerous radioactivity, every reactor core is surrounded by two containment vessels (see Fig. 5.10).

The only nuclear power plant to have suffered a meltdown leading to the release of substantial amounts of radioactivity is the unit at Windscale, England. The graphite moderator of the Windscale reactor caught fire, causing some of the fuel elements to melt. A considerable amount of radioactive iodine (^{131}I) was spread over the countryside and contaminated crops and milk supplies. The Windscale

Figure 5.10 Cutaway view of a nuclear power plant. The reactor is in the center. Notice the control rods that enter the reactor through the top and the airtight door that leads to the interior of the large outer containment vessel. The large pipes carry steam to the turbines on either side of the reactor. The man in the lower right has been included to give an indication of the scale. [Courtesy of Combustion Engineering, Inc.]

reactor did not have an outer protective container, but all of the reactors in U.S. nuclear electric stations do have containment vessels. The only other meltdown to have occurred in a commercial power plant took place in 1966 at the Enrico Fermi reactor, 18 miles downriver from Detroit. The containment vessel was not breached and no serious leakage of radioactivity occurred, although the reactor was rendered unserviceable for a considerable period of time.

Reactor engineers have been exceedingly conservative in the design of the safety features in nuclear reactors. All of the parts that are subject to high pressure or high temperatures are rated far in excess of the operating values. Every control circuit has at least one backup system and usually more than one. There is an emergency cooling system which comes into operation if the primary system fails or is overloaded. And, finally, in the event of some unforeseen difficulty, the reactor will *fail-safe* and shut down. The likelihood of an explosion or a melt-down has been reduced to a very low level but, of course, these disasters are always *possibilities*. Critics have charged that insufficient attention has been given to the improvement of reactor safety measures, particularly those relating to possible meltdowns. Nevertheless, the nuclear power industry has a better safety record than any other major industry.

2. *Radioactive Emissions*. Every reactor in normal operation releases small amounts of radioactivity into the atmosphere. Maximum limits have been set for the amount of radioactivity that any reactor can emit and most reactors release far less than the limit. But no amount of radioactivity moving freely through the air is "good," and efforts are continuing to reduce these emissions to the absolute minimum. At the present level of emission, persons living near nuclear power plants receive considerably less radiation from the plant than they do from other sources (cosmic rays, medical X rays, color TV sets, and so forth). Critics contend that even this small increment in the level of radiation is unwarranted and leads to increased danger of leukemia and other radiation-induced cancers. Nuclear proponents admit that all radiation is dangerous to humans but that the small increases caused by reactor operations pose such a tiny additional health hazard that the benefits far outweigh the risks.

Even a coal-burning power plant releases some radioactivity into the air due to the occurrence in the coal supply of minerals that contain radioactive elements, particularly radium. These emissions often exceed those of nuclear power plants in normal operation.

3. Fuel Processing. In the course of normal operations, the fuel rods in a reactor undergo various changes and after a time must be replaced with new rods. When safety or reduced power output dictates the removal of a rod, it contains, in addition to the radioactive fission fragments, a substantial fraction of the original uranium or plutonium. After a "cooling off" period, during which the short-lived radioactivity decays, the used fuel rods are shipped to a processing plant where the remaining fuel is removed by chemical separation methods. Those radioactive isotopes that are useful in medical, industrial, and research applications are separated and prepared in convenient forms. The remaining radioactive material is put into a form suitable for disposal (see below). All of this handling of the "hot" fuel rods must be carried out remotely behind thick shielding walls. Close controls are necessary to ensure that any radioactivity released during processing operations is held to minimum levels.

4. Disposal of Radioactive Wastes. Although much of the material in used fuel rods is recovered in the processing operation, there remains a quantity of radioactive "garbage" that is not particularly useful. As more and more nuclear power plants become operational, these materials accumulate at an increasing rate. The safe disposal of radioactive wastes represents a serious problem because some of the isotopes have half-lives of hundreds or thousands of years. Various methods of disposal have been used. The earliest was simply to dump steel containers of the wastes at sea. But the containers corroded and eventually leaked the radioactivity into the water. The practice of disposal at sea has now been halted.

We have found no really acceptable long-term solution to the disposal problem, and radioactive wastes are now stored in liquid form in huge million-gallon tanks in concrete-shielded underground bunkers (see Fig. 5.11). Because of the corrosion problem, the storage sites are continuously monitored for leaks and the highly radioactive material is transferred periodically to new

Figure 5.11 Two of the 30 high-level radioactive waste storage tanks at the Atomic Energy Commission's Savannah River Plant in South Carolina, shown here under construction in 1972. The tanks are now surrounded by concrete and dirt and contain 1,000,000 gallons each of reactor wastes. [Courtesy of E. I. du Pont de Nemours & Co., S.C.]

containers. At the present time, nearly 100 million gallons of radioactive wastes from reactors are stored in this way.

It has been proposed that radioactive wastes be deposited in abandoned salt mines. One of the main problems in waste disposal is to ensure that the radioactivity does not enter a water system that eventually connects with the population's supply. Because salt is quite soluble in water, the existence of salt deposits indicates that little or no water seeps through the region. A salt-mine depository should therefore ensure that the radioactivity will not enter the underground water system.

Although such a plan appears reasonable, there are many uncertainties—for example, oil wells or dry holes that penetrate the salt deposit might connect with water-bearing layers and could conceivably flood the mine. Radioactive material might then be carried away to the water supply of a nearby town or city. Consequently, the proposals for underground storage of radioactive wastes in salt mines as well as in rock layers are still under study and are directed toward finding a site with no possible connections to the local water system. One promising site is a 4000-ft-thick salt deposit in southeastern New Mexico. This salt layer has few penetrations and is being actively studied as a possible waste disposal site. It appears that salt deposits offer the best possibility for the long-term storage for radioactive wastes with the minimum of necessary surveillance.

5. Thermal Pollution. Any electrical generating plant that uses steam to drive turbines must have a cooling system to condense the steam back into water. The cooling system necessarily exhausts heat into a water system or into the air. In this regard, a nuclear power plant is no different from a coal-burning plant—both systems release excess heat into the environment, thus causing *thermal pollution*. Because nuclear power plants are, at present, less efficient than coal-burning plants (32 percent compared to 40 percent), a nuclear plant will exhaust about 1.5 times as much heat to the environment as will a coal-burning plant with the same power output.

If the heat is exhausted into a moving water system (a river or a bay), there will be an increase in the water temperature that is measurable for some distance downstream. The amount of temperature increase depends on the power level of the plant, the energy conversion efficiency, and the flow rate of the water reservoir. Extensive studies have shown no drastic changes in the marine ecology downstream from reactor sites although some changes in the populations of marine life forms have been noted.

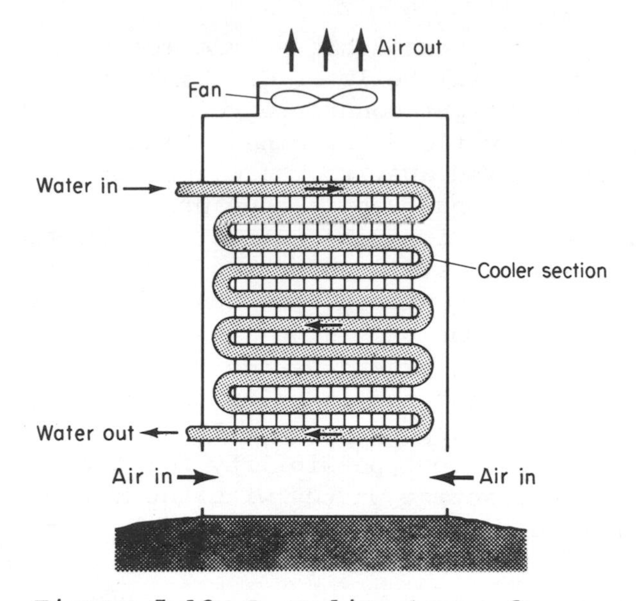

Figure 5.12 A cooling tower for removing heat from the water in the cooling loop of a steam power plant (either nuclear or coal burning).

Instead of exhausting heat into a water reservoir, a *cooling tower* can be used to dissipate the heat into the atmosphere. One type of cooling tower is shown in Fig. 5.12 (see also Fig. 5.13). Air is pulled up through the tower by large fans and this continual flow of air removes heat from the water in the reactor's cooling loop. Although exhausting heat into the atmosphere does influence to some extent the local weather conditions downwind, it is generally believed that cooling tower systems perturb the environment less severely than systems which exhaust into water reservoirs. About one-sixth of the U.S. electrical generating plants (500 MWe and larger) now use cooling towers. This fraction will increase as acceptable sites for natural water cooling decrease due to water availability and more stringent environmental controls.

The operation of nuclear power plants certainly involves risks. But almost every aspect of our modern technological society—airplane or automobile travel, handling electrical

Figure 5.13 The Calder Hall Nuclear Power Station in England. Four giant cooling towers exhaust the surplus heat into the atmosphere. The plumes are condensed water vapor (literally, clouds). [United Kingdom Atomic Energy Authority]

equipment, even crossing the street—involves a certain risk. The important issue is whether the benefits are worth the risk. One particularly striking way to set forth the risk factor involved with the use of nuclear power is to estimate the number of deaths that might result from nuclear radiations associated with power plant operations. Ralph Lapp has analyzed the situation and tabulated the number of deaths expected in the United States due to radiation-induced cancers during the period from 1972 to 2000. His results are shown in Table 5.2. It can be seen that less than one radiation-cancer death in 3000 is attributable to radiation from nuclear power operations.

TABLE 5.2
Deaths Expected in the United States due to Radiation-Induced Cancer in the Period 1972-2000[a]

Source of radiation	Expected deaths
Natural background	200,000
Medical X rays	100,000
Cosmic rays received during jet travel	7,200
Fallout from weapons tests	6,800
Nuclear power plants	90
	314,090

[a]After R. E. Lapp.

In terms of benefit versus risk, the evidence that we now have appears to favor nuclear power. But this is no reason to ignore the possible risks nor to cease efforts to improve reactor safety. Indeed, safety research is a large part of the on-going nuclear power program.

It is interesting to note that the conversion from conventional (fossil) methods of producing power to nuclear generators has proceeded much more smoothly in the United Kingdom than in the United States. Nuclear power plants have met with widespread public acceptance in Britain, due in part to the fact that the alternatives based on coal and oil are politically and economically less desirable.

NUCLEAR FUSION

When a heavy nucleus such as uranium undergoes fission, energy is released because the binding energy per particle is greater for the fission fragments than for the original nucleus. In fact, energy will be released in *any* type of nuclear process which results in an *increase* of the binding energy. How can we take advantage of this fact in a process other than fission? Referring to Fig. 5.3, we see that the binding energy per particle increases with mass number for A less than about 50. Therefore, if we bring together two light nuclei to form a more massive nucleus with $A < 50$, energy will be liberated in the reaction. For example, when two deuterium nuclei combine to form a helium nucleus, approximately 24 MeV of energy is released:

$$^{2}H + ^{2}H \rightarrow ^{4}He + 24\ \text{MeV} \tag{5.11}$$

Reactions in which two light nuclei combine and release energy are called *fusion reactions* (the nuclei *fuse* together).

Actually, when two deuterium nuclei collide and interact, the production of ^{4}He is relatively unlikely. It is much more probable that a reaction will take place which produces either a proton or a neutron:

$$^{2}H + ^{2}H \rightarrow ^{3}H + ^{1}H + 4.0\ \text{MeV} \tag{5.12a}$$

or,

$$^{2}H + ^{2}H \rightarrow ^{3}He + n + 3.3\ \text{MeV} \tag{5.12b}$$

That is, in the $^{2}H + ^{2}H$ reactions, approximately 1 MeV of energy is released for each of the four particles involved. This is about the same efficiency of mass-to-energy conversion that occurs in fission (approximately 200 MeV for the 236 particles involved in ^{235}U + n fission).

Although both release energy, the fission and fusion processes differ in a significant respect. In the fission case, the electrical repulsion that exists between the two parts of the nucleus which become fission fragments *assists* in breaking the nucleus apart. In a fusion reaction, on the other hand, the electrical repulsion between the two nuclei *resists* their combining into a single nucleus. Consequently, a fusion reaction between two deuterium nuclei will take place only if the nuclei are projected toward one another with high speeds.

How can we produce high-speed collisions between deuterium nuclei? One way would be to use some sort of accelerator (for example, a cyclotron) to project deuterium nuclei onto a deuterium target. In fact, this technique has been extensively used to study the $^{2}H + {}^{2}H$ reactions. But such a method is not practical if we expect to produce useful amounts of fusion energy. Another way is to take advantage of the fact that the atoms in a gas are continually in motion—if we need high speeds, we raise the temperature. However, in order to achieve the high speeds that are necessary to produce fusion reactions among deuterium atoms, a temperature of about 10 million degrees centigrade is needed! Reactions that require these extraordinarily high temperatures are called *thermonuclear reactions*.

The interior of the Sun is at a sufficiently high temperature that fusion reactions take place. Indeed, the Sun's source of energy is the fusing together of hydrogen in the core to produce helium. On the Earth, thermonuclear temperatures can be generated in the explosions of nuclear fission devices. The *hydrogen bomb* operates on this principle—a fission device serves as a high-temperature trigger to induce the fusion of hydrogen isotopes (deuterium and tritium) with the release of enormous amounts of energy. A hydrogen bomb (or *thermonuclear bomb*) can be constructed to yield considerably more energy than would be practical with a weapon that uses only the fission of uranium or plutonium.

There are two different reaction cycles that are proposed for fusion reactors. One involves the use only of deuterium as fuel. Because of the enormous supply of deuterium in the oceans, the fuel for this system is essentially limitless. In the other scheme, lithium (actually, the isotope ^{6}Li) is required in addition to deuterium. Although lithium must be mined from deposits in the Earth's crust, the potential supply is very large and should last for 100,000 years or more, even at high consumption rates. In both of the proposed fusion cycles there is no limit to the fuel supply in the foreseeable future.

The first of the fusion cycles is the *deuterium-deuterium* scheme. In this system, deuterium nuclei react with one another to produce ^{3}He and ^{3}H nuclei, according to Eqs. 5.12, with the release of energy. Furthermore, deuterium nuclei also react with the ^{3}H (tritium) nuclei produced in the first step to release even more energy. The reactions, and their equivalent sum, are

$$^{2}H + {}^{2}H \longrightarrow {}^{3}H + {}^{1}H + 4.0 \text{ MeV}$$

$$^{2}H + {}^{2}H \longrightarrow {}^{3}He + n + 3.3 \text{ MeV}$$

$$^{2}H + {}^{3}H \longrightarrow {}^{4}He + n + 17.6 \text{ MeV}$$

$$5\,{}^{2}H \longrightarrow {}^{4}He + {}^{3}He + {}^{1}H + 2n + 24.9 \text{ MeV} \qquad (5.13)$$

Thus, in this series of reactions the tritium that is produced is subsequently consumed (in large measure) with the release of additional fusion energy.

In the second series of reactions, lithium is used as a breeder material to produce tritium—this is the *deuterium-lithium* cycle:

$$^{6}Li + n \longrightarrow {}^{4}He + {}^{3}H + 4.8 \text{ MeV}$$

$$^{2}H + {}^{3}H \longrightarrow {}^{4}He + n + 17.6 \text{ MeV}$$

$$^{6}Li + {}^{2}H \longrightarrow 2\,{}^{4}He + 22.4 \text{ MeV} \qquad (5.14)$$

In the deuterium-deuterium cycle, the reactants are in the form of a high-temperature ionized gas or *plasma*. In the deuterium-lithium cycle, some method must be devised to provide a layer of molten lithium to absorb the neutrons and produce tritium.

FUSION REACTORS—PROSPECT FOR THE FUTURE

The fantastic potential that fusion reactions have for the production of useful energy has been known for many years, but the technical problems in building a practical

Figure 5.14 Tokamak. The Soviet Tokamak device for the magnetic confinement of hot plasmas. [TASS from SOVFOTO]

fusion reactor are much more complex than those involved in fission reactors. How can a plasma at 10,000,000°K be confined and controlled so that thermonuclear energy is made available at a steady rate? Several methods are being investigated. One is to confine the plasma in a magnetic field while the nuclei interact. An experimental facility of this type, the Soviet "Tokamak," is shown in Fig. 5.14. Similar machines have been constructed in the United States and in Europe. The large new devices are inching closer to the conditions under which the amount of energy released in fusion reactions is equal to the energy required to heat and confine the plasma. Of course, this "break even" point must be far exceeded before a fusion reactor will produce useful amounts of power.

Another approach to the fusion problem is being pursued vigorously by groups in this country and in the Soviet Union. In this scheme a tiny pellet of fusion material (for example, solid deuterium and tritium surrounded by a casing) is bombarded from all sides with powerful laser bursts. The incident radiation causes some of the exterior material to vaporize and to be blown off. The reaction to this ablation is that a shock wave moves from the surface of the pellet toward the center, compressing the deuterium and tritium to higher and higher densities. A sufficiently intense shock wave (this means a sufficiently powerful burst of laser radiation) should bring the nuclei close enough so that fusion will take place. Indeed, neutrons have been detected coming from the pellets in some recent experiments, thus demonstrating that a compression to fusion densities has been achieved.

One proposal for incorporating this technique into a power-producing fusion reactor is shown in the sketch in Fig. 5.15. The laser radiation is split into several beams and is guided by mirrors (not shown) into the reaction chamber through several ports. The solid pellets are formed by the cryogenic (low-temperature) unit at the top of the chamber and fall to the center where they are blasted by the precisely timed laser beams. Neutrons emitted in the fusion reactions are absorbed in the liquid lithium layer that surrounds the reaction chamber. Neutron absorption in lithium produces nuclear reactions which heat the lithium. The hot lithium is pumped through a heat exchanger where water is converted into steam. The remainder of the power plant is the same as in conventional or fission generating plants, namely, the steam turns turbines which are connected to electrical generators.

Do the recent experiments constitute a real "breakthrough" in fusion research? Are we close to the realization of cheap, abundant fusion power? We may know the answers

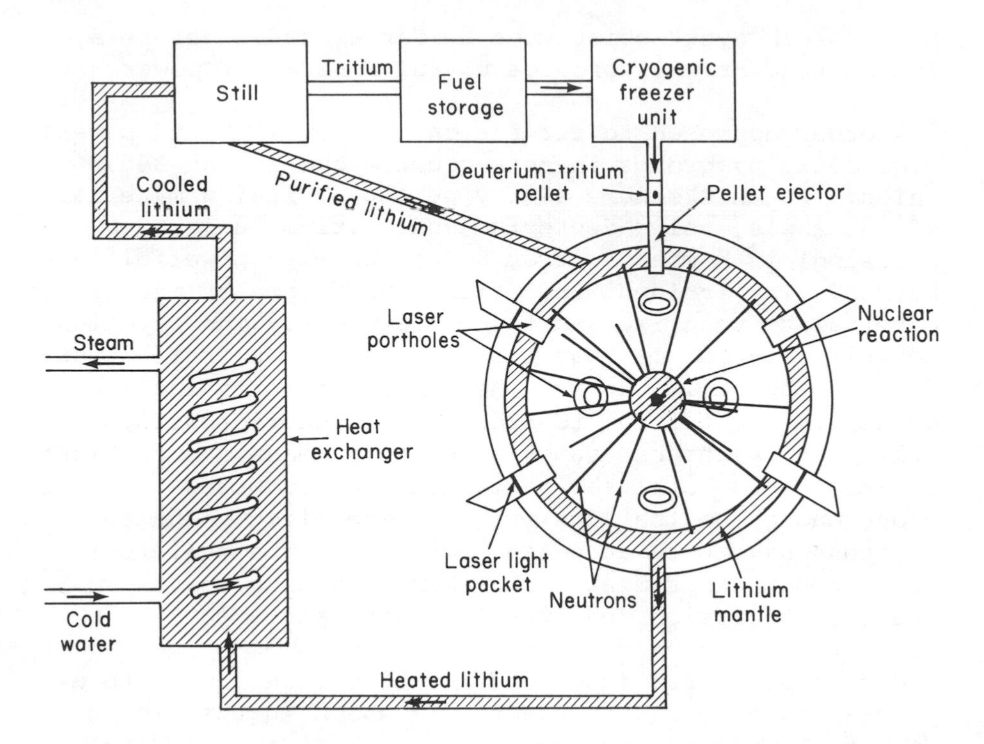

Figure 5.15 One of the proposals for the construction of a fusion power plant utilizing laser-induced fusion.

to these questions within a few years. But the most optimistic hope is that a fusion power plant will be in operation by 1990. The widespread use of energy from nuclear fusion will probably be achieved only in the next century.

There are many advantages to fusion-produced power. The fuel supply is plentiful and relatively inexpensive. Moreover, the products of fusion reactions are either stable isotopes or they are only weakly radioactive. Radioactivity will also be produced by the neutrons released in the reactions when they are captured in the materials of the reactor. But even so, the amount of radioactivity associated with the operation of a fusion reactor will be only a small fraction of that produced in the several phases of fission reactor operations. One of the most serious problems is the fact that large amounts of tritium (^3H) will be produced in fusion reactors. Although tritium is only weakly radioactive, its chemical behavior is exactly the same as ordinary hydrogen and it can readily enter into organic substances. Control of tritium will be one of the major problems in the operation of fusion reactors.

THERMONUCLEAR FISSION—A NEW TWIST ON NUCLEAR ENERGY

Apart from the technological problems of constructing a power-producing fusion reactor, there are two main difficulties with the fusion process as a practical source of power. The first is that the fusion reactions $^2H + ^2H$ and $^2H + ^3H$ produce neutrons. In order to utilize the kinetic energy of these neutrons, they must be slowed down in some material, thereby causing the material to become heated; the extraction of this heat energy is an inefficient process. Second, the slow neutrons are absorbed by the reactor materials which then become radioactive. Radioactivity is also present in the form of tritium (^3H), which will be produced in massive quantities in fusion reactors. There would be substantial advantages if a nuclear reaction were used in which only charged particles are emitted and which leaves no radioactive residue.

It has recently been proposed that the boron-plus-hydrogen reaction could be used to meet these criteria. In this reaction, the nucleus ^{11}B combines with a proton to produce three ^4He nuclei (α particles):

$$^{11}B + ^1H \longrightarrow ^4He + ^4He + ^4He + 8.7 \text{ MeV} \quad (5.15)$$

This reaction is radically different from those that have been proposed for use in fusion reactors. Usually, it is possible to extract energy from nuclei only when a heavy nucleus undergoes fission or when two light nuclei undergo fusion. The boron-plus-hydrogen reaction, however, is really a fission process involving a light nucleus. Ordinarily such a process requires the input of energy. But because the end products of the $^{11}B + ^{1}H$ reaction are tightly bound helium nuclei, this reaction actually releases energy.

Boron is a plentiful element (found in the oceans and in dry lake beds), and so there is an abundant fuel supply. The primary difficulty is that the $^{11}B + ^{1}H$ reaction requires a substantially higher temperature for ignition (about 3×10^9°C) than do the reactions involving deuterium. (This is because of the greater nuclear charge of the boron nucleus.) However, these extremely high temperatures can probably be developed eventually in laser-compressed pellets. The high-temperature fission of boron has been termed *thermonuclear fission*.

In a "conventional" fusion reactor, the neutrons are trapped and their kinetic energy is converted into heat for the purpose of boiling water to drive a steam generator. Because the products of the $^{11}B + ^{1}H$ reaction are rapidly moving charged particles, they automatically represent an electrical current and this can be converted directly into useful output power without the necessity of a thermal cycle. Moreover, the products of boron fission are not radioactive. (Some radioactivity will be produced in secondary reactions initiated by the fast α particles emitted in boron fission, but the amount should be only about 0.1 percent of that produced in a deuterium fusion reactor operating at the same power level.)

Although the thermonuclear fission of boron may not be attempted until the deuterium systems are thoroughly explored, this new idea is potentially of great importance in the eventual generation of clean, inexpensive nuclear power.

QUESTIONS AND EXERCISES

1. The nucleus of ^{7}Li consists of 3 protons and 4 neutrons. Could ^{7}Li exist if its mass were equal to 3 proton masses plus 4 neutron masses? Explain.

2. The mass of a helium nucleus is 4.0016 AMU. What is the binding energy per particle for ^{4}He?

3. Would energy be released by the fission of a nucleus with $A = 60$ into two equally massive fragments? (Refer to Fig. 5.3.)

4. The energy release in the detonation of 1 ton (2000 lb) of TNT is approximately 4×10^9 J. Express the energy released in the fission of 1 kg of ^{235}U in terms of tons of TNT. It has become common practice to express the yields of fission weapons in terms of tons (or kilotons) of TNT and the yields of thermonuclear weapons in terms of megatons of TNT. H-bombs with yields in excess of 100 megatons have been constructed.

5. In Fig. 5.7, notice that the water which passes through the reactor core does not also pass through the turbine. Instead, the heat is transferred to a second water loop which is entirely outside the reactor. Why is this done?

6. Why have nuclear-powered submarines been so successful and yet the only nuclear-powered freighter (the *Savannah*) has been retired while still in good condition? (Consider the mission of a submarine compared to that of a freighter. Which type of vessel is at sea for long periods of time?)

7. All elements with atomic number Z greater than 83 are radioactive. (Uranium, $Z = 92$, is radioactive, but the half-lives of the isotopes ^{235}U and ^{238}U are sufficiently long that uranium occurs naturally in the Earth.) Some of these high-Z elements are found

in uranium ores. Are there likely to be any hazards associated with the residues of material (the *tailings*) that result from extracting uranium from its ore?

8. Benefit versus risk is an important consideration in determining whether to expand the nuclear power industry. How do you feel about the benefit versus risk in having a chest X ray?

9. Would you rather build a home on a riverbank downstream from a large dam or near a nuclear power plant? Is your offhand answer based on knowledge of the relative probabilities of accidents or on emotion? Has emotion been a factor in any of the statements you have heard about the energy crisis, or have all of the statements been based on thorough studies?

10. In order to be practical, a fusion reactor must produce more energy than it uses. What are some of the ways in which energy must be used to operate a fusion reactor?

APPENDIX. ON THE FEASIBILITY OF COAL-DRIVEN POWER STATIONS*

The following article is reprinted from the Yearbook of the Royal Institute for the Utilization of Energy Sources for the Year MMMMCMLV, p. 1001.

In view of the acute crisis caused by the threat of exhaustion of uranium and thorium from the Earth and Moon Mining System, the Editors thought it advisable to give the new information contained in the article the widest possible distribution.

---

*Article by O. R. Frisch. Originally appeared in *The Journal of Jocular Physics,* Vol. 3, pp. 27-30, in commemoration of the 70th birthday of Professor Niels Bohr (October 7, 1955) at the Institutet for Teoretick Fysick, Copenhagen. Reprinted by permission of the author.

Introduction. The recent discovery of coal (black fossilized plant remains) in a number of places offers an interesting alternative to the production of power from fission. Some of the places where coal has been found show indeed signs of previous exploitation by prehistoric men who, however, probably used it for jewels and to blacken their faces at tribal ceremonies.

The power potentialities depend on the fact that coal can be readily oxidized, with the production of a high temperature and an energy of about 0.0000001 megawattday per gramme. This is, of course, very little, but large amounts of coal (perhaps millions of tons) appear to be available.

The chief advantage is that the critical amount is very much smaller for coal than for any fissile material. Fission plants become, as is well known, uneconomical below 50 megawatts, and a coal-driven plant may be competitive for isolated communities with small power requirements.

Design of a Coal Reactor. The main problem is to achieve free, yet controlled, access of oxygen to the fuel elements. The kinetics of the coal-oxygen reaction are much more complicated than fission kinetics, and not yet completely understood. A differential equation which approximates the behaviour of the reaction has been set up, but its solution is possible only in the simplest cases.

It is therefore proposed to make the reaction vessel in the form of a cylinder, with perforated walls to allow the combustion gases to escape. A concentric inner cylinder, also perforated, serves to introduce the oxygen, while the fuel elements are placed between the two cylinders. The necessary presence of end plates poses a difficult but not insoluble mathematical problem.

Fuel Elements. It is likely that these will be easier to manufacture than in the case of fission reactors. Canning is unnecessary and indeed undesirable since it would make it impossible for the oxygen to gain access to the fuel. Various lattices have been calculated, and it appears that the simplest of all—a close packing of equal spheres—is likely to be satisfactory. Computations are in progress to determine the optimum size of the spheres and the required tolerances. Coal is soft and easy to machine; so the manufacture of the spheres should present no major problem.

Oxidant. Pure oxygen is of course ideal but costly; it is therefore proposed to use air in the first place. However it must be remembered that air contains 78 per cent of nitrogen. If even a fraction of that combined with the carbon of the coal to form the highly toxic gas cyanogens this would constitute a grave health hazard (see below).

Operation and Control. To start the reaction one requires a fairly high temperature of about 988°F; this is most conveniently achieved by passing an electric current between the inner and outer cylinder (the end plates being made of insulating ceramic). A current of several thousand amps is needed, at some 30 volts, and the required large storage battery will add substantially to the cost of the installation.

There is the possibility of starting the reaction by some auxiliary self-starting reaction, such as that between phosphine and hydrogen peroxide; this is being looked into.

Once the reaction is started its rate can be controlled by adjusting the rate at which oxygen is admitted; this is almost as simple as the use of control rods in a conventional fission reactor.

Corrosion. The walls of the reactor must withstand a temperature of well over a 1000°F in the presence of oxygen, nitrogen, carbon monoxide and dioxide, as well as small amounts of sulphur dioxide and other impurities, some still unknown. Few metals or ceramics can resist such gruelling conditions. Niobium with a thin lining of nickel might be an attractive possibility, but probably solid nickel will have to be used. For the ceramic, fused thoria appears to be the best bet.

Health Hazards. The main health hazard is attached to the gaseous waste products. They contain not only carbon monoxide and sulphur dioxide (both highly toxic) but also a number of carcinogenic compounds such as phenanthrene and others. To discharge those into the air is impossible; it would cause the tolerance level to be exceeded for several miles around the reactor.

It is therefore necessary to collect the gaseous waste in suitable containers, pending chemical detoxification. Alternatively the waste might be mixed with hydrogen and filled into large balloons which are subsequently released.

The solid waste products will have to be removed at frequent intervals (perhaps as often as daily!), but the health hazards involved in that operation can easily be minimized by the use of conventional remote-handling equipment. The waste could then be taken out to sea and dumped.

There is a possibility—though it may seem remote—that the oxygen supply may get out of control; this would lead to melting of the entire reactor and the liberation of vast amounts of toxic gases. Here is a grave argument against the use of coal and in favour of fission reactors which have proved their complete safety over a period of several thousand years. It will probably take decades before a control system of sufficient reliability can be evolved to allay the fears of those to whom the safety of our people is entrusted.

Chapter 6
THE EFFECTS OF NUCLEAR RADIATIONS

Nuclear reactors are now providing us with much needed electrical power, and they are building up larger and larger residues of radioactive wastes. There appears to be no possibility, at least in the short term, that nuclear reactors will "go away." However, it does seem possible to alter the rate at which nuclear power facilities are constructed. Should we push for a more rapid change to nuclear power in order to save our fossil fuels and to decrease air pollution? Or should we insist on a slower move to nuclear power in order to decrease the potential hazards of the accidental release of radioactive materials into the environment?

We can form opinions on these questions only if we have some knowledge of radioactivity and the effects that nuclear radiations can have on Man and his environment. In this chapter we examine the various kinds of radiations that are emitted by radioactive substances, and we discuss the net results—both "bad" and "good"—that can come from utilizing radiation.

THE DISCOVERY OF RADIOACTIVITY

In 1896 an important discovery was made, quite by accident, by the French physicist Henri Becquerel. Becquerel found that when he placed a sample of uranium salts (potassium uranyl sulfate) on a piece of unexposed photographic film, the developed film revealed an outline of the salt crystals. The same result was obtained even when the film was wrapped in heavy black paper, a sufficient shield to exclude all light from the film. Furthermore, the darkening of the film was observed when *any* substance containing uranium was placed on the film. Clearly, it was uranium, and not light, that had caused the film to show an outline of the crystals, and Becquerel reasoned that the uranium must be emitting some different kind of radiation, rays that had not been detected before. This new phenomenon was called *radioactivity*.

Before the end of the nineteenth century, the study of radioactivity had led to the discovery of two new elements. In 1897 Marie Curie selected as her doctoral research problem the investigation of the mysterious rays emitted by uranium. In order to determine whether elements other than uranium produced these rays, Madame Curie tested every known element. Only two were found to be radioactive—uranium and thorium. We now know that a larger number of elements exhibit radioactivity in their natural forms, but these activities are weak and Madame Curie's methods were not sufficiently sensitive to detect their presence. She used various materials in her experiments, sometimes pure elements and sometimes minerals. One curious fact emerged—the mineral *pitchblende* (an ore of uranium) was a much more prolific source of radiation than was pure uranium metal. Since pitchblende contained no thorium, Madame Curie wondered whether there could be an undiscovered element, an impurity in the pitchblende, that could account for the exceptional radioactivity of this ore. She then began a series of tedious chemical procedures designed to isolate the source of the intense radioactivity in pitchblende. By the end of 1898, Marie Curie and her husband Pierre (neither of whom were chemists) had succeeded in preparing two tiny samples of highly radioactive substances which they had laboriously separated from pitchblende. All tests showed that these substances were not compounds but new elements. The Curies named their elements *polonium* and *radium*.

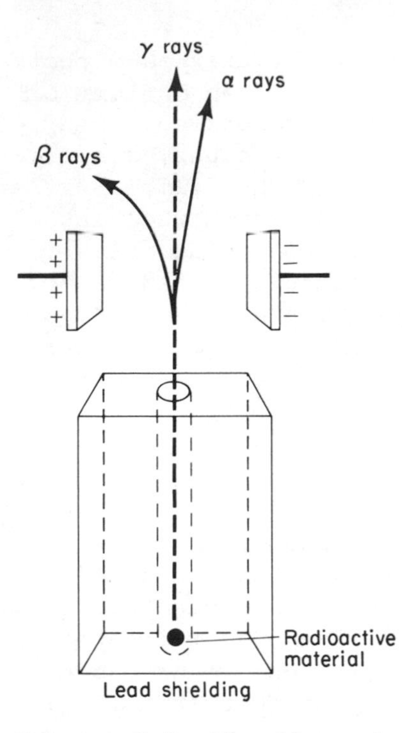

Figure 6.1 The three types of radiations emitted by a radioactive sample are affected in different ways by an electric field. The bending of the β rays toward the positive plate shows that these particles are negatively *charged. Similarly, the bending of the α rays in the opposite direction shows that these particles are* positively *charged. (The less massive β particles are bent by a much greater amount than the α particles.) Gamma rays are unaffected by the electric field; they are* neutral *rays.*

Within a few years after the Curies' discoveries, three different types of emanations from radium and other radioactive substances had been identified. For lack of any better names for these new radiations, they were labeled by the first three letters of the Greek alphabet, designations that we still use:

(a) *Alpha rays* are positively charged particles with relatively large mass.

(b) *Beta rays* are negatively charged particles with mass much less than that of alpha rays.

(c) *Gamma rays* are neutral rays with no detectable mass.

Alpha rays and beta rays (or α particles and β particles) were studied by bending the particles in an electric field (Fig. 6.1) and by measuring the buildup of electrical charge on surface or wires that collected the radiation. These experiments showed that β particles are identical to *electrons* and that α particles are the same as *helium nuclei* (that is, helium atoms from which two electrons have been removed). Gamma (γ) rays proved to be identical to X rays and light, except that their frequencies are much higher.

NUCLEAR CHANGES

Radioactivity is a *nuclear* phenomenon and it does not depend in any way on chemical or physical changes that the *atom* may undergo. The rate and the speed with which α particles are emitted from radium are the same whether the radium is in the form of the pure metal or whether it is in a chemical compound. Radioactivity is unaffected by temperature, pressure, or chemical form (except to a very small extent in special circumstances).

When an α particle, a β particle, or a γ ray is emitted by a radioactive substance, it emerges from the *nucleus* of the material. But the electron structure of an atom depends on the amount of electrical charge in the nucleus. Consequently, if there is a change in the nuclear charge, there will be a corresponding change in the number of atomic electrons. For example, the radium nucleus ($Z = 88$, $A = 226$) has 88 protons and 138 neutrons. When ^{226}Ra emits an α particle (^{4}He), two protons and two neutrons are carried away (Fig. 6.2). Therefore, the residual nucleus has 86 protons and 136 neutrons. The product of radium α decay (the *daughter*) is a different element—*radon* ($Z = 86$). The atomic electron structure changes, following the decay event, to accommodate the new nuclear

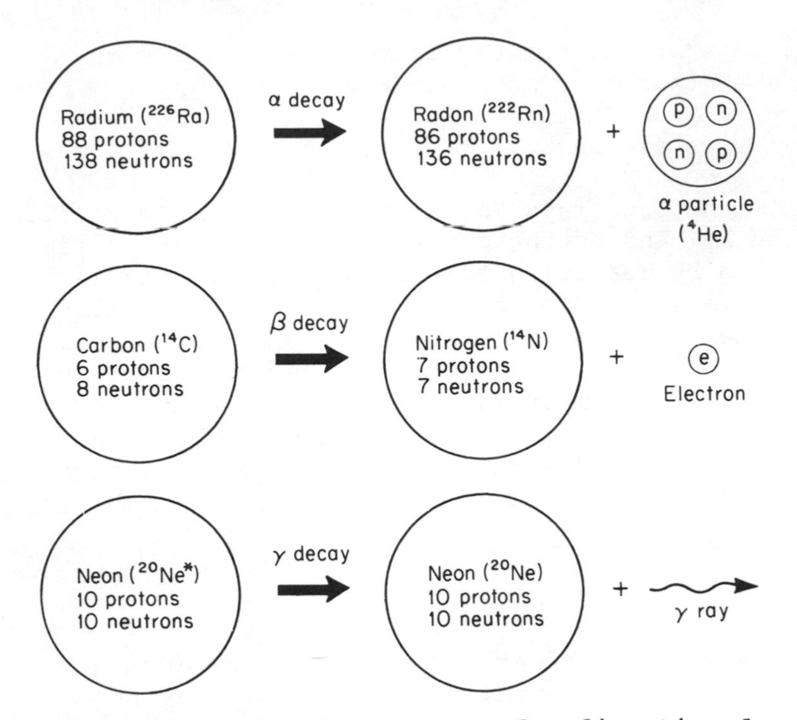

Figure 6.2 The three types of radioactive decay process. Alpha and beta decay are nuclear disintegration events in which the original nucleus changes into a different species. Gamma radiation usually follows α and β decay as the protons and neutrons of the daughter nucleus rearrange themselves; no disintegration process is involved in the emission of γ rays. (The excited nucleus that exists before γ-ray emission takes place is represented by an asterisk.)

charge by releasing two of its 88 electrons. These two electrons, or their equivalent, eventually attach themselves to the emitted α particle and form a neutral atom of ^{4}He. Thus the original neutral radium atom decays and two neutral atoms are formed, one of radon and one of helium.

In the β decay process, an electron is emitted from the nucleus. (But this electron does not preexist in the nucleus; the electron is formed in the β decay process

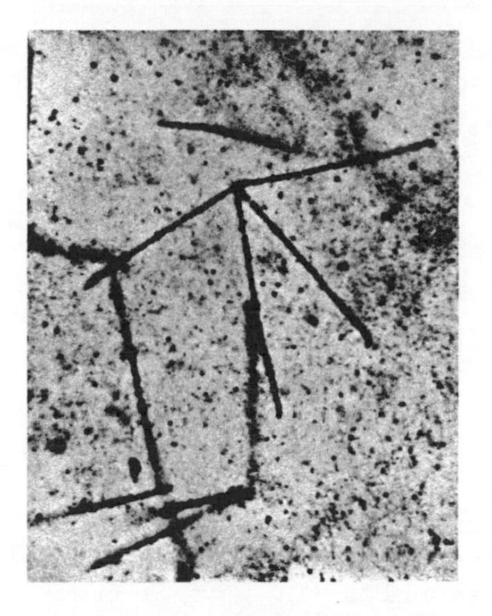

Figure 6.3 The path traveled by a single *nuclear particle can be recorded by using a special photographic film (called a* nuclear emulsion*). This photomicrograph shows the tracks left by several α particles emitted from a single radioactive parent nucleus and its radioactive daughters. In this process, a thorium nucleus emits an α particle, leaving a radioactive daughter nucleus; this nucleus emits another α particle, again leaving a radioactive nucleus; and so on. The length of the longest track in this picture is approximately* 3×10^{-5} m, *or* 0.03 mm. *[Courtesy of Wills Physical Laboratory.]*

and is immediately ejected.) The removal of a negative charge from the nucleus means that the (positive) nuclear charge *increases* by one unit (that is, by +e). Thus, a nucleus with atomic number Z that undergoes β decay becomes a nucleus with atomic number $Z + 1$. But no proton or neutron is emitted in a β radioactivity process and so the mass number A of the daughter nucleus is the same as the mass number of the parent nucleus. When radioactive ^{14}C (6 protons, 8 neutrons) emits a β particle, the new nucleus contains 7 protons and 7 neutrons—that is, ^{14}N is formed (Fig. 6.2).

The α decay of ^{226}Ra and the β decay of ^{14}C can be represented by the following schematic nuclear "equations":

$$^{226}_{88}Ra \xrightarrow{\alpha \text{ decay}} {}^{222}_{86}Rn + {}^{4}_{2}He$$
$$^{14}_{6}C \xrightarrow{\beta \text{ decay}} {}^{14}_{7}N + {}^{0}_{-1}e \qquad (6.1)$$

where we use the nuclear notation to show that the electron has $A = 0$ and $Z = -1$.

In *stable* nuclei (those that do not exhibit radioactivity) the protons and neutrons exist together permanently with no changes. However, if a neutron is removed from a nucleus (by means of a nuclear reaction) and becomes a *free* neutron, it cannot exist permanently. In fact, a free neutron undergoes exactly the same kind of β decay as does a radioactive nucleus such as ^{14}C:

$$^{0}_{0}n \longrightarrow {}^{1}_{1}H + {}^{0}_{-1}e \qquad (6.2)$$

Indeed, we can view radioactive β decay as a process in which one *nuclear* neutron changes into a proton (with the accompanying emission of an electron). This is exactly the process by which ^{14}C is converted into ^{14}N (see Fig. 6.2).

Two important facts about radioactive decay processes should be noted:

(a) The total number of protons and neutrons present before the decay takes place is exactly equal to the number after the decay. For example, the mass number of ^{226}Ra (226) equals the sum of the mass numbers of ^{222}Rn and ^{4}He (222 + 4); and similarly for the β decay of ^{14}C.

(b) The total electrical charge is the same before and after the decay takes place. For example, in the α decay of ^{226}Ra, there are 88 protons present before decay and

86 + 2 after decay. In the β decay of ^{14}C, there are 6 protons present before decay and 7 protons afterward; but an electron is also present after decay, so there is a balance of electrical charge [6e = 7e + (-e)].

THE HALF-LIFE

An atom of radioactive carbon (^{14}C) can undergo β decay and become an atom of nitrogen (^{14}N). But what happens to a sample of ^{14}C, consisting of a large number of atoms, as time goes on? The sample does not suddenly become ^{14}N. Nor does the amount of ^{14}C decrease uniformly to zero after some period of time. Instead, the process of radioactive decay obeys a different kind of law. Every radioactive species has associated with it a characteristic time, which is called the *half-life* and is denoted by the symbol $\tau_{\frac{1}{2}}$. The half-life has the following significance. Suppose that we begin with a sample of ^{14}C consisting of N_0 atoms. After a time $\tau_{\frac{1}{2}}$ (which for ^{14}C is 5730 years) one-half of the ^{14}C atoms will have decayed and the sample will consist of 1/2 N_0 atoms of ^{14}C and an equal number of ^{14}N atoms (Fig. 6.4).

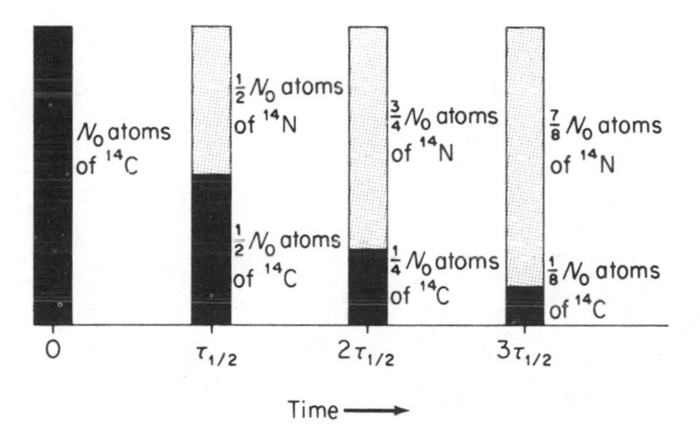

Figure 6.4 The radioactive decay law for the case of the $^{14}C \longrightarrow {}^{14}N$ decay. In each interval of time $\tau_{\frac{1}{2}}$, the number of atoms of ^{14}C surviving is equal to one-half the number that existed at the beginning of that interval.

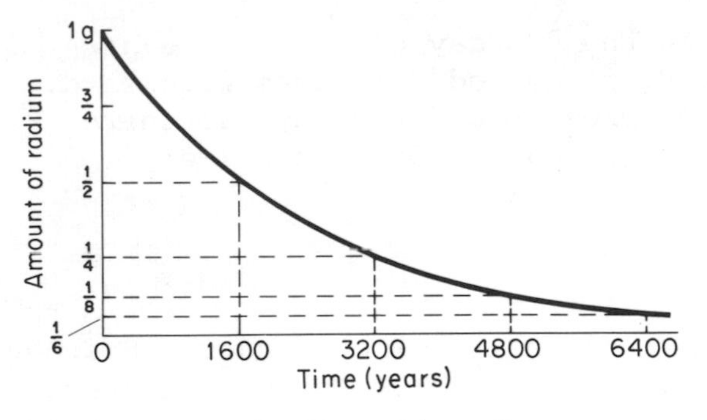

Figure 6.5 Radioactive decay curve for ^{226}Ra. The half-life is approximately 1600 years.

What happens during the time from $\tau_{\frac{1}{2}}$ to $2\tau_{\frac{1}{2}}$? We can apply the same reasoning as before. We start with 1/2 N_0 atoms of ^{14}C at time $\tau_{\frac{1}{2}}$, so after an interval of one half-life (that is, at the time $2\tau_{\frac{1}{2}}$), one-half of the sample with which we started will have decayed. Therefore, at time $2\tau_{\frac{1}{2}}$, we will have remaining only 1/4 N_0 atoms of ^{14}C and there will be 3/4 N_0 atoms of ^{14}N. Similarly at time $3\tau_{\frac{1}{2}}$, we will have 1/8 N_0 atoms of ^{14}C. In every interval of time $\tau_{\frac{1}{2}}$, the sample will decrease by 1/2.

Figure 6.5 shows the way in which a sample of radium (^{226}Ra) decreases with time. The half-life of radium is approximately 1600 years. Therefore, if we start with 1 gram of ^{226}Ra, after 1600 years 1/2 gram of radium will remain, after 3200 years (that is, an additional half-life) 1/4 gram will remain, after 4800 years 1/8 gram will remain, and so on.

The range of known half-lives for α and β decay extends from a small fraction of a second to many billions of years. Some typical values are listed in Table 6.1.

THE INTERACTION OF RADIATION WITH MATTER

In the different radioactive decay processes, α particles (^{4}He nuclei), β particles (electrons), and γ rays (high-energy photons) are emitted. What happens when these

TABLE 6.1
Some Radioactive Half-Lives

Nucleus	Type of decay	Half-life
Thorium (^{232}Th)	α	1.41×10^{10} y
Radium (^{226}Ra)	α	1602 y
Plutonium (^{238}Pu)	α	87.4 y
Polonium (^{214}Po)	α	1.64×10^{-4} s
Potassium (^{40}K)	β	1.28×10^{9} y
Carbon (^{14}C)	β	5730 y
Cobalt (^{60}Co)	β	5.26 y
Neutron (^{0}n)	β	760 s
Krypton (^{93}Kr)	β	1.29 s

radiations strike and interact with matter? When an α or a β particle or a γ ray enters a piece of matter, energy is transferred to the material through collisions with the atoms in the material. These interactions lead to the ejection of electrons from the atoms and therefore produce ions in the material. If the material is sufficiently thin or if the radiation has a high energy, the particle or ray can pass completely through the material, losing only a portion of its original energy; otherwise, the particle or ray will be absorbed within the material and will lose all of its energy through ionization. (Alpha, beta, and gamma rays are collectively called *ionizing radiations*.) This ionization, in turn, gives rise to chemical reactions and to a general heating of the absorbing material. It is the ionization produced in matter that makes these radiations useful in a variety of practical situations, and makes them dangerous if they enter the body.

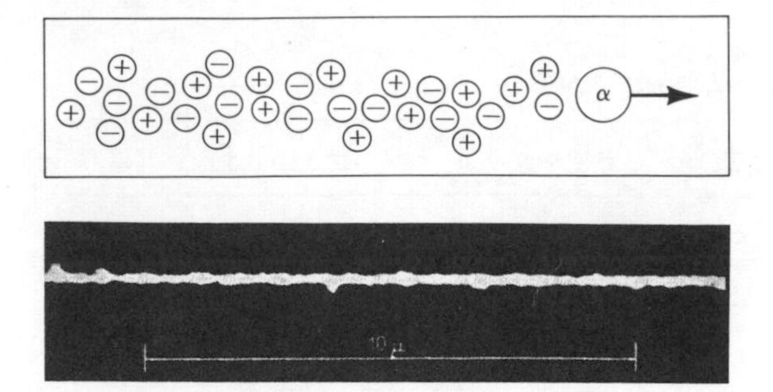

Figure 6.6 An α particle passing through matter leaving a large number of ions in its path. (Below) Photograph of the track of an α particle in a cloud chamber. The white streak consists of tiny water droplets that condense on the ions produced by the α particle. (One micron (1 μ) is equal to 10^{-6} m.) [Photograph reprinted with permission from an article by R. H. Johnsen in Chemistry, *July-August 1967, p. 35. Copyright by the American Chemical Society.]*

When an α particle passes through matter, the double nuclear charge (+2e) causes intense ionization along its path. Furthermore, because an α particle is so much more massive than an electron, the ionization encounters (which involve electrons) do not appreciably deflect the α particle from its original direction of motion. As a result, an α particle plows almost straight through matter, leaving a high density of ions in its wake (Fig. 6.6). Because of the extremely small size of a nucleus compared to that of an atom, ionization events are much more likely than nuclear collisions. An α particle traveling through matter will produce many millions of ions for each nuclear collision.

An electron, on the other hand, because of its small mass and single electrical charge, leaves behind far fewer ions per centimeter traveled and is frequently deflected in the electron collisions. The ionization produced by an electron is much more diffuse than that produced by an α particle (Fig. 6.7). Consequently, an electron can penetrate much deeper into matter than can an α particle with the same energy. An α particle with 5 MeV (a typical energy for α particles from radioactive materials)

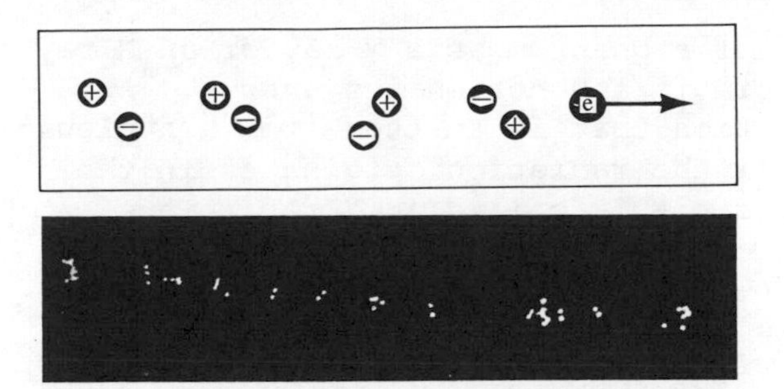

Figure 6.7 When an electron (or β particle) passes through matter, it leaves behind only scattered ions. (Below) Cloud chamber track of an electron, showing the low density of ions. (Compare Fig. 6.6b.) [Photograph reprinted with permission from the same article by R. H. Johnsen. Copyright by the American Chemical Society.]

will be stopped by a sheet of paper, but a 5-MeV electron will penetrate about an inch of biological material.

When a γ ray passes through matter, it can be completely absorbed and an energetic electron is ejected from an atom: This is the *photoelectric effect*. Or the γ ray can be deflected by an atomic electron, transferring to the electron some of its energy: This is the *Compton effect*. The γ ray is not absorbed in this process and it continues on to interact again with some other electron. Therefore, the ionization produced by a γ ray is due to the electrons that are released from atoms and has the characteristics of electron ionization described above. [Gamma rays with energies greater than 1 MeV can interact with matter to produce electron-positron (e^--e^+) pairs, but we are not concerned with this type of interaction here.]

Gamma rays are high-energy electromagnetic radiations and, except for energy, are identical with X rays, light photons, and radio waves. For most radiation applications, high energy is required; therefore, in this chapter we discuss only γ rays and X rays, and are not concerned with lower energy radiations.

The classification of a quantum as a γ ray or an X ray depends only on its origin and not on its energy. Any electromagnetic radiation that is emitted from a nucleus is called a γ ray. If the radiation originates in the atomic electron shells, it is called an X ray. Thus, a 20-keV γ ray and a 20-keV X ray could be emitted from the same atom and the radiations would be exactly the same.

Gamma rays from radioactive decay processes result only in the deexcitation of a nucleus that is left in an excited energy state following α or β decay (see Fig. 6.2). Radioactive decay involving only γ radiation does not occur.

NEUTRONS

Neutrons are not emitted in radioactive decay events, but neutrons can be produced in nuclear reactions initiated by high-energy particles in accelerator beams. A variety of target materials will yield neutrons when bombarded by high-speed particles. For example, the bombardment of lithium by protons produces neutrons according to the reaction

$$^{7}Li + ^{1}H \longrightarrow ^{7}Be + n \tag{6.3}$$

The absence of electrical charge makes the neutron an interesting and important particle. When a neutron strikes a piece of matter, it does not interact with the atomic electrons (this happens only with *charged* particles); instead, neutrons interact with the *nuclei*. These neutron-nucleus interactions can result in the transfer of energy from the neutron to the nucleus (see the discussion of neutron moderators in the preceding chapter), or in a neutron-induced disintegration. The capture of a neutron by a nucleus often results in the formation of a radioactive isotope. (In the case of a heavy nucleus, the result can be fission.)

In traveling through a piece of matter, a neutron does not produce any ionization. When the neutron strikes a nucleus, the nucleus recoils as a result of the collision. As the nucleus moves through the surrounding atoms, some of the atomic electrons are stripped away. Thus the collision produces ionization along the path of the recoiling nucleus. In a material that contains a large fraction of hydrogen (for example, biological tissue), neutrons interact primarily with the nuclear protons of the hydrogen atoms. The knocked-on protons are the particles that produce almost all of the ionization in such materials.

RADIATION UNITS

In order to specify the amount of radioactivity contained in a sample and the amount of radiation absorbed by an object, we make use of two units—the *curie* (Ci) and the *rad*. A curie of radioactivity represents 3.7×10^{10} decay events per second (regardless of the type or energy of the radiation). The curie is named for Marie and Pierre Curie who discovered radium. Originally, one curie (1 Ci) meant the number of disintegrations per second taking place in one gram of radium, but the definition has been broadened and standardized to mean *exactly* 3.7×10^{10} disintegrations per second of any radioactive material. Standard laboratory sources are usually near 10^{-6} Ci or 1 μCi (microcurie); sources used in industrial processing (for example, ^{60}Co) frequently are 10^3 Ci = 1 kCi (kilocurie) and sometimes are as large as 10^6 Ci = 1 MCi (megacurie).

The *rad* is a unit that specifies the amount of radiation energy absorbed by an object. A dose of one rad corresponds to the absorption of 0.01 joule per kilogram of material:

$$1 \text{ rad} = 0.01 \text{ J/kg} \qquad (6.4)$$

Radiation doses up to 10^7 rad (10 Mrad) are commonly delivered to materials in industrial applications. If a person were to stand 1 m away from a 1-Ci source of

^{60}Co for 1 hr, he would receive a dose of approximately 1.2 rad at the front surface of his body and a dose of about half this amount at a depth of 10 cm because of the attenuation of the γ rays in passing through the body tissue. As we will see later in this chapter, there are no immediately detectable effects in humans of radiation doses below about 25 rad. However, even small doses of radiation are suspected of being harmful in some degree. Therefore, extreme caution should be exercised whenever a radiation source is in the vicinity, and no exposure should be tolerated unless it is necessary to derive some benefit.

RADIOACTIVITY PRODUCED BY REACTORS

During its normal operations, a nuclear power reactor produces substantial quantities of radioactivity. Some of the radioisotopes have short half-lives (a few days or less) and decay quickly, even before the fuel rods are processed. Many of the isotopes that are produced, however, have half-lives ranging from tens to millions of years. These radioisotopes are the ones that are responsible for the problem of waste disposal. Table 6.2 lists the long-lived reactor-produced activities and the amounts of activity in curies produced by a typical large power reactor. The total amount of radioactivity produced per year of operation amounts to more than 5 megacuries (5 MCi).

As we have already mentioned, nuclear wastes are now stored primarily in liquid form in heavily shielded underground tanks. When suitable deep storage sites are identified and approved, the procedure will change. The nonvolatile elements—Sr, Cs, I, Tc, Pu, Am, and Cm—will be cast in a ceramic material and stored underground as solids. The gaseous elements—krypton and tritium—will be handled differently because they could escape from a ceramic casting. ^{85}Kr will be held as a gas and ^{3}H will be held as tritiated water in special containers until they decay. This procedure is possible because both of these radioisotopes have comparatively short half-lives (see Table 6.2).

TABLE 6.2
Long-Lived Activities Produced by a Reactor Operating at 3000 MWt (1000 MWe)[a]

Isotope	Half-life (years)	Curies of activity produced per year
^{137}Cs	30.0	2,790,000
^{90}Sr	28.1	2,000,000
^{85}Kr	10.8	285,000
^{244}Cm	17.6	64,500
^{3}H	12.3	18,000
^{241}Am	458	4,650
^{238}Pu	86	2,700
^{243}Am	8.0×10^3	465
^{99}Tc	2.1×10^5	375
^{240}Pu	6.6×10^3	120
^{239}Pu	2.4×10^4	45
^{129}I	1.7×10^7	1
		5.2 MCi

[a]Adapted from A. M. Weinberg and R. P. Hammond.

How much radioactivity will eventually be produced by reactors in the United States? The projection shown in Fig. 3.5 indicates that we will need about 15×10^{12} kWh of electrical energy in the year 2000. This corresponds to an average power of 1.7×10^6 MWe. If we assume a plant efficiency factor of 60 percent to allow for peak load conditions and adequate reserves, the necessary installed capacity will be 2.8×10^6 MWe. Let us further assume that 50 percent of this power (1.4×10^6 MWe) will be furnished by nuclear reactors. If the average capacity of each nuclear plant is 1000 MWe, we will need 1400 plants to meet the anticipated power demand. (One AEC study indicates that we will need 2000 breeder reactors by the year 2020.) With each reactor producing 5.2 MCi of radioactivity each year, the annual total will be about 7300 MCi in the year 2000.

This calculation raises two questions (at least). What will we do with 7300 MCi of radioactivity each year? Where will we *put* 1400 nuclear power stations? The first question is easier to answer than the second. If we store our radioactive wastes in underground salt deposits, only a few square miles will be required to accommodate a year's output of reactor-produced activity. And there are at least 500,000 square miles of available salt deposits in the United States. Not all of these deposits may be suitable as depositories for radioactive wastes, but it appears that we can develop suitable sites for the storage of many years of accumulated activity. The disposal of radioactive wastes presents an enormous long-term burden. For many thousands of years, the future generations must maintain and monitor these depositories of radioactive materials. This is a situation that has never before confronted Man. Can proper maintenance be continued without incident for millennia? Or could some break in the long chain of responsibility lead to the disastrous release of radioactivity?

If we decide to build 1400 nuclear plants, it is unlikely that they will be scattered around the country in 1400 individual sites. Instead, we will probably concentrate the reactors in a smaller number of "nuclear parks" which will be capable of producing 40,000 MWe or so of electrical power. One advantage of this system is that the processing of fuel rods will be economically feasible on the site, thus eliminating the necessity for transporting the used rods to a central facility. If these parks could be located over salt deposits, the entire operation of handling and storing radioactivity could be carried out in a restricted area. One other possibility that has been proposed is to cluster several reactors at offshore sites and to suspend them several hundred feet beneath the surface of the sea. The ocean water would then provide shielding from the radiations produced and would permit cooling of the reactor cores without significant thermal pollution (if carefully designed).

Of course, the larger questions are as follows: Do we really want several thousand reactors around? Can we tolerate the increased risk of a nuclear accident? Do we want the responsibility of producing billions of curies of radioactive wastes that must be contained and continually monitored for thousands of years? Perhaps this is part of the price we must pay for our lavish use of energy.

RADIATION DAMAGE IN BIOLOGICAL SYSTEMS

Every person on Earth is continually exposed to various kinds of radiation from many different sources. Ordinarily, these radiations do us no particular harm. But even the most familiar of radiations—solar radiation—can do damage to the skin or eyes if the exposure is too great. Infrared radiation from a heat lamp or ultraviolet radiation from a "sun lamp" can also cause uncomfortable burns (even serious burns) if used carelessly. However, when we use the term *radiation damage,* we usually mean the injurious effects that are caused by radiations of higher energy. In this category are X rays from medical or dental X-ray units and television sets, as well as α, β, and γ radiations from natural or artificial radioactive sources and from accelerators that produce nuclear radiations. The reason for this distinction is that radiations such as ultraviolet and infrared rays have very low penetrating power. Therefore, these radiations are stopped by the outer layers of skin and any damage that results from excessive exposure is superficial. On the other hand, X rays and, particularly, γ rays can easily penetrate the body and can damage the internal organs. Although a severe sunburn can be extremely painful, we do not ordinarily classify this annoyance as "radiation damage." (However, repeated excessive exposure to solar radiation can produce skin cancers.)

Almost all of the radiation that is capable of producing biological damage and to which the general public is exposed is in the form of X or γ radiation. Persons who work with radioactivity or with accelerators are sometimes exposed to α and β particles or to other high-speed nuclear particles. All of these radiations produce ionization in matter and can therefore inflict damage on biological tissue.

When considering the biological effects of radiation, it is important to remember that the unit of absorbed dose—the *rad*—refers to the energy absorbed per kilogram. Therefore, the amount of radiation energy absorbed by a 100-kg man who receives a *whole-body* dose of 1 rad is much greater than if he receives a 1-rad dose only to his arm. On the other hand, if the same amount of *energy* is absorbed by the arm or by the body as a whole, the dose in rads is much less in the latter case.

RELATIVE BIOLOGICAL EFFECTIVENESS AND THE REM

It has been found that equal absorbed doses delivered by different types of ionizing radiations will produce varying amounts of biological damage. Thus, an individual who receives a whole-body dose of 1 rad due to high-speed α particles will suffer considerably more tissue damage than if he receives the same whole-body dose of 200-keV X rays. We say that α particles have a greater *relative biological effectiveness* (RBE) than low-energy X rays. Compared to 200-keV X rays (which are defined to have an RBE of 1), the RBE of α particles is approximately 20. Approximate RBE values for the more common radiations are given in Table 6.3. These values are only approximate because the biological effectiveness of a particle or ray depends to some extent on its energy. Nevertheless, the tabulated values serve as useful guides to the effectiveness of the different radiations.

Fast neutrons produce radiation damage in tissue primarily through the protons that they set into motion because of collisions. Slow neutrons, on the other hand,

TABLE 6.3
Relative Biological Effectiveness of Various Radiations

Radiation	RBE value (approximate)
X or gamma ray	1
Electrons (beta particles)	1
Alpha particles	20
Protons	10
Fast neutrons	10
Slow neutrons	5

have very little energy to impart to protons; nevertheless, they can produce high-energy secondary radiations by inducing nuclear reactions.

Because of the differing biological effectiveness of different types of radiation, the *rad* (which measures only the total energy deposited per unit mass of the absorber) is not a useful unit for indicating radiation damage in living matter. Instead, a unit called the *rem* is used. This unit measures the energy deposited per unit mass multiplied by the RBE of the particular radiation—that is, the *equivalent dose:*

$$1 \text{ rem} = (1 \text{ rad}) \times (\text{RBE}) \tag{6.5}$$

Thus, if a person receives a 0.2-rad dose of α particles (a substantial dose!), the exposure is measured as (0.2 rad) × (20) = 4 rem. If the exposure is entirely to X and γ radiation or electrons, the dose equivalent in rem is equal to the dose in rad.

RADIATION EXPOSURE

The largest contribution to the radiation received by an individual who is not a radiation worker is from natural sources—cosmic rays and the radioactivity that occurs in the Earth. The amount of natural radiation received during the course of a year by a particular

RADIATION AREA

Figure 6.8 This symbol is universally used to indicate an area where radioactivity is being handled or artificial radiations are being produced.

individual depends on his location and habits. Some parts of the country have more natural radioactivity than others; the intensity of cosmic radiation depends on altitude—the residents of Denver receive 50 percent more cosmic radiation than the residents of San Francisco; some wristwatches have luminous dials that contain radium; and so forth. The range of natural radiation doses received by individuals in the United States is approximately 90 to 150 mrem per year (1 mrem = 1 millirem = 10^{-3} rem).

The second most significant source of radiation exposure is medical and dental X rays. (We include here only routine diagnostic X rays; therapeutic treatments are special situations.) Again, there is a wide variation among individuals—some persons may have no X rays whereas others may require extensive sets of X rays for the diagnosis of particular medical problems. The normal range of exposure (in the United States) from this source is 50 to 100 mrem per year.

The radioactive fallout from weapons tests amounts to about 5 mrem per year. *If* an agreement to stop all testing is reached, this figure will decrease gradually with time because of the decay of the radioactive residue still present in the atmosphere from previous tests. (The United States, Great Britain, and the Soviet Union have discontinued atmospheric testing, but China, France, and India still carry out such tests.)

The remaining source of radiation exposure—that due to the operation of nuclear power reactors—is the most controversial of all. Averaged over the entire U.S. population, the individual exposure is about 0.003 mrem per year at present. But if a person were to live for the entire year on the downwind boundary of one of the older nuclear plants (where the radiation containment is not as effective as for the newer plants), the exposure could amount to 5 mrem per year. Of course, in the unlikely event of a catastrophic accident (and this is the point of controversy), the exposure could be considerably higher. For comparison, it is interesting to note that a transcontinental trip by air typically exposes a passenger to a radiation dose greater than 0.01 mrem due to the effects of cosmic rays.

A summary of exposure figures for the U.S. population is given in Table 6.4.

TABLE 6.4
Radiation Exposure of Individuals in the United States

	Dose range (mrem/y)	Average dose in U.S. (mrem/y)
Natural (cosmic rays, radioactivity)	90-150	102
Medical and dental X rays (diagnostic only)	50-100	76
Weapons tests fallout	5	4
Nuclear power plant operation	<0.01-5	0.003[a]
Total	145-260	182

[a]Increasing to about 3 mrem per year by the year 2000.

EFFECTS OF RADIATION DAMAGE

What does radiation actually *do* to a person? Radiation effects can be divided into two categories: (a) effects on the individual exposed (*somatic* effects), and (b) effects on the offspring of the individual exposed (*genetic* effects). We can also divide the type of exposure into two categories: (a) long-term, or *chronic*, exposure at a relatively constant level, and (b) single-dose, or *acute*, exposure which is all received in a short time. Not all radiation damage is cumulative, so an individual may exhibit no somatic effects if exposed to 40 rem of radiation when the dose is distributed uniformly over a 40-year period. However, if a person received a 40-rem dose all at once, he would develop some of the symptoms of *radiation sickness*, but full recovery would be expected.

There are no immediately detectable somatic effects of acute exposure at dose levels below about 25 rem. However, there are *delayed* effects such as increased susceptibility to leukemia, bone cancer, and eye cataracts, as well as a shortened lifespan. In a sample of one million people, about 100 cases of leukemia will develop each year. If every person in this sample were to receive a 1-rem dose of radiation, an additional one to two cases of leukemia would be expected to develop during the following year. The shortening of lifespan due to radiation exposure is estimated to be 10 days/rem for acute exposure and 2.5 days/rem for chronic exposure. (Some estimates are even smaller.) Thus, the person referred to in the previous paragraph who received a single-dose, whole-body exposure of 40 rem, developed some symptoms of radiation sickness, and then recovered, would have a life expectancy up to 1 year shorter than normal. If the 40-rem dose resulted from chronic (instead of acute) exposure, the individual's life expectancy might be shortened by about 3 months.

Acute doses of more than a few hundred rem result in violent sickness and even death. The somatic effects of various levels of radiation exposure are summarized in Table 6.5.

TABLE 6.5
Somatic Effects of Radiation Exposure

Whole-body dose (rem)	Effects	Remarks
0-25	None detectable	
25-100	Some changes in blood, but no great discomfort; mild nausea	Some damage to bone marrow, lymph nodes, and spleen
100-300	Blood changes, vomiting, fatigue, generally poor feeling	Complete recovery expected; antibiotic treatment
300-600	Above effects plus infection, hemorrhaging, temporary sterility	Treatment involves blood transfusions and antibiotics; severe case may require bone marrow transplants. Expected recovery about 50 percent at 500 rem
>600	Above effects plus damage to central nervous system	Death inevitable if dose >800 rem

The genetic effects of human exposure to radiation are much more subtle than somatic effects; we still know relatively few details about the way in which the hereditary information carried in molecules of DNA is affected by radiation. Although many experiments have been carried out using insects and animals, the results are not directly applicable to the human case. Extensive studies have also been made on the survivors of the Hiroshima and Nagasaki blasts and their offspring, but too few generations have passed to assess the lasting genetic effects. Such observations are made especially difficult because some birth defects are due to causes other than radiation and because some of the radiation-induced mutations are due to natural radiation.

PUBLIC EXPOSURE TO RADIATION

As far as most somatic effects are concerned (at least for adults), the damage resulting from many small doses appears to be *less* than that resulting from a single large dose because the body has an opportunity to recover from small doses spaced in time. The evidence indicates that this is not true for genetic effects (and probably for some somatic effects such as leukemia susceptibility). Thus there is no level of radiation exposure below which there is zero damage to humans. All radiation is harmful to some extent. There is no argument on this point; but there is a continuing debate as to the amount of damage produced by small doses accumulated at low rates. The discussion centers around whether the benefits of radiation-producing devices, such as nuclear power plants, outweigh the increased risks of the resulting radiation exposure, even though for the *average* citizen this risk is small.

At the present time, the policy is to acknowledge that there are decided benefits in various operations that involve the production and use of radiation, so that *some* exposure of the general public is inevitable. It is also recognized that the exposure, especially to those who do not work with radiation and who may be unaware of any radiation in their environment, must be kept to the absolute minimum. Currently, the maximum permissible amount of radiation to which a typical individual may be exposed is set at 170 mrem per year over and above the dose due to natural radiations. It is estimated that this level of exposure would not unduly burden the population in terms of increased radiation risks.

There are opponents to this view, however, and they argue that steps should be taken to lower the amount of nonnatural radiation to which the population is exposed. This could be accomplished in a number of ways—for example, by stopping the testing of nuclear devices of any kind, by using diagnostic X rays only when absolutely required, by placing more stringent regulations on the allowable radiation from television sets and microwave cooking ovens, and by halting the proliferation of nuclear power plants. Some of these measures appear to be desirable steps, whereas the population may be unwilling to accept the additional inconvenience and expense associated with others.

THE OTHER SIDE OF THE COIN

Lest the reader be left with the impression that all nuclear radiations are "bad," brief mention should be made of the fact that these radiations have been used

Figure 6.9 The effect of radiation as a food preservative technique is strikingly illustrated in these photographs. The potato at the bottom was irradiated with 20,000 rad of ^{60}Co γ *rays; the top potato was not treated. After storage for 16 months the untreated potato had developed an appreciable sprout structure, whereas the irradiated potato was still firm, fresh-looking, edible, and had no sprouts. [Courtesy of Brookhaven National Laboratory.]*

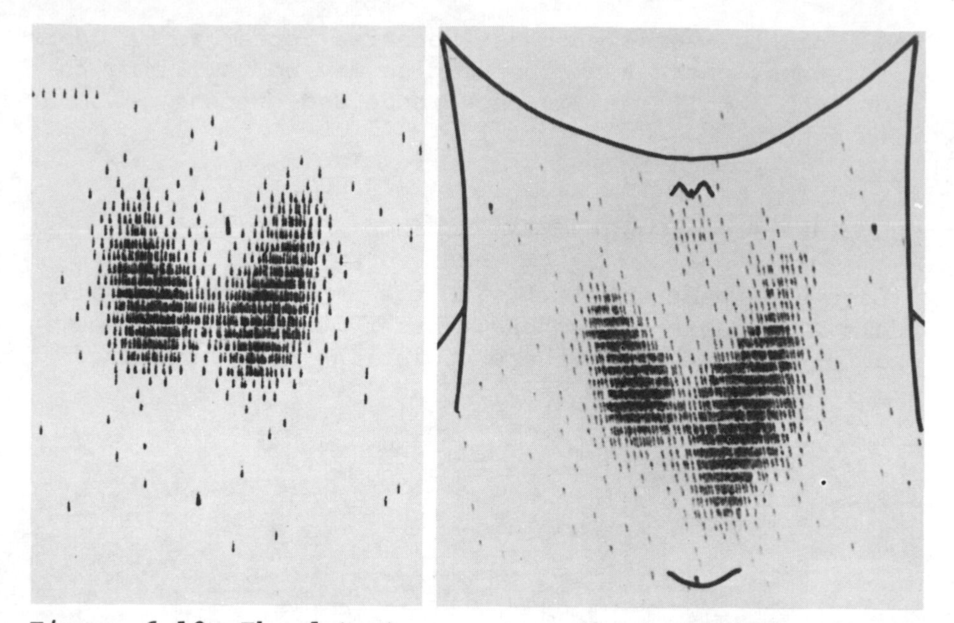

Figure 6.10 The detector scan on the left shows the distribution of ^{131}I in a normal thyroid gland. The scan on the right shows the result obtained for a cancerous gland. [Courtesy of Oak Ridge National Laboratory.]

in many ways for the benefit of Mankind. Many of the radioisotopes that are used in research, in medical applications, and in industry are produced in nuclear reactors.

Item. Nuclear radiation is routinely used to alter the molecular structures of various plastic materials and thereby produce more durable and heat-resistant materials.

Item. Radiation methods are used in the textile industry to fix various chemicals onto cotton fibers which gives the product permanent-press and soil-release properties.

Item. Certain types of medical supplies are sterilized by exposure to penetrating radiation.

Item. Some foodstuffs are given increased shelf life by irradiations that kill the microorganisms which cause food spoilage (see Fig. 6.9).

Item. Several different industries use nuclear radiations to monitor items on production lines and individually control the quality of every item.

Item. Many bulky industrial items cannot be examined conveniently using X-ray techniques, whereas nuclear radiations permit the internal structures to be checked (nuclear *radiography*).

Item. Radioisotope tracer studies have permitted biochemists to learn more in the last 20 years about the functioning of living things than had been discovered in the previous two centuries.

Item. Radioisotopes are routinely used in many types of medical diagnostic examinations (see Fig. 6.10).

Item. Various types of cancers can be successfully treated by using radiation techniques with external sources or with specific radioisotopes that are administered internally.

QUESTIONS AND EXERCISES

1. A radiation detector is used to measure the activity of a sample of ^{90}Sr. It is found that the sample undergoes 8×10^8 decays in 1 hr. What is the activity of the sample (in microcuries)?

2. The half-life of ^{131}I is 8 days. On a certain day, the activity of an ^{131}I sample is 6.4 mCi. What will be the activity of the sample 40 days later?

3. How many α particles are emitted per day by a sample of polonium which has an activity of 1 nCi (10^{-9} curie)?

4. How much greater will be the radiation damage produced by a number of 3-MeV protons compared to that produced by an equal number of 1-MeV β particles?

5. One individual receives a whole-body dose of 10 rad of γ radiation and another individual receives a whole-body dose of 700 mrem of α particles. Which individual will suffer the greater radiation damage?

6. Speculate as to the long-term effects on the population if there were no controls on the use of radiation or the release of radioactivity into the atmosphere. How might the *gene pool* of the human race be affected?

7. Radium, thorium, and radioactive potassium (^{40}K) are found in small quantities in the materials from which bricks and concrete are made. Therefore, the radiation level in a brick-and-concrete house is generally higher than in a house constructed from wood. Do you believe that the radiation risk is worth the benefit of the increased insulation qualities and decreased fire hazard in a brick-and-concrete house compared to a frame dwelling?

8. The process of *evolution* (or *natural selection*) involves the carrying forward into future generations of characteristics or traits that result from mutations and give the individual some sort of competitive advantage over those not possessing these traits. Giraffes, for example, evolved long necks in order to reach leaves high on trees that could not be eaten by other animals. Because radiation is capable of producing mutations through ionizing changes in DNA, can it be argued that increased radiation is therefore *good*?

9. Radiation-induced mutations can be produced in grains, fruits, and other crops by irradiating the seeds from which the plants grow. What kind of mutations in wheat, for example, would be desirable and should be cultivated?

10. Some elements, when taken into the body, deposit selectively in certain organs or certain regions of the body. Iodine, for example, is concentrated in

the thyroid gland and calcium is concentrated in the bones and teeth. Suppose that a certain radiation worker ingests a small speck of a radioisotope that is deposited exclusively and uniformly in the bone marrow. The total mass of the worker's bone marrow is 1 kg. The material emits 5-MeV α particles and the ingested sample has an activity of 10 nCi (10^{-8} curie). Assume that none of the sample is eliminated but instead resides permanently in the body. If the particular radioisotope has a long half-life (as does radium, for example), the activity will remain essentially constant for many years. What dose will the individual's bone marrow have received in 1 year? (Ans. 18 rem.)

Chapter 7
ENERGY AND THE ENVIRONMENT

Every month we pay our fuel bills (or *energy* bills). We receive accountings for our use of electricity, oil, and natural gas in our homes and for the gasoline used in our automobiles. And there are indirect charges that we pay for the energy used in manufacturing processes and for the transportation of goods that we buy.

We pay for the energy we use not only in terms of the direct and indirect charges for electricity and fuel consumption but also in terms of the effects that energy production has on our world (Fig. 7.1). It is not possible to place a dollar value on many of the side effects associated with energy production. What is the value of the health impairment caused by automobile exhaust fumes? What value do we place on the destruction of farmland and the pollution of water caused by the strip mining for coal? What value is associated with the loss of seaside beaches because of oil spills washing ashore?

Modern society cannot exist without the production and utilization of energy. And as long as we continue to use fuels, there will necessarily be undesirable side effects. We must pay a price for energy. How much are we willing to pay?

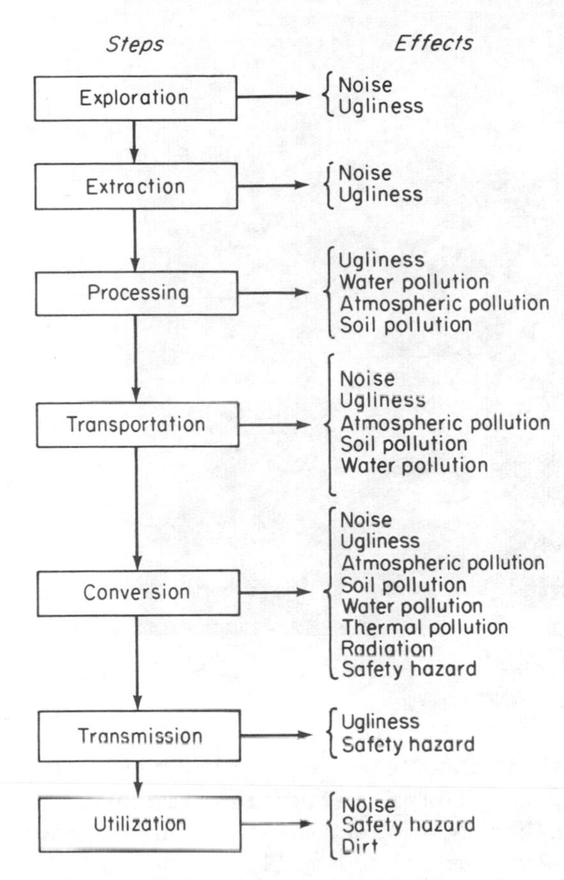

Figure 7.1 Steps in the production and utilization of energy together with the associated effects on the world. Each step also involves thermal *pollution. [After Ali Bulent Cambel.]*

THE EFFECTS OF WATER POWER

We often think of electrical energy generated by hydroelectric power plants as the least offensive of the various energy-producing systems in use today. But there are serious problems associated with the construction of giant dams on natural waterways. A case in point is the Aswan High Dam on the Nile River in southern Egypt (Fig. 7.2). For thousands of years the annual floods of the Nile have been carrying silt from the African highlands to revitalize

Figure 7.2 The old and the new at the Aswan High Dam in Egypt. [NOVOSTI from SOVFOTO.]

the soil along the banks of the Nile, virtually the only cultivatable land in Egypt. The flood waters flushed away the soil salts that had been accumulated during the previous year and annually dumped 130 million tons of rich sediment into the Mediterranean Sea, adding to the food chain of marine life and helping to maintain the proper salinity in the entire eastern end of the Mediterranean.

The presence of the Aswan High Dam has changed all this. Without the Nile sediment flowing into the Mediterranean, the plankton and organic carbons, vital to the marine life, have been reduced by one-third. The number of fish in the area has been drastically diminished, with some species having been forced into other waters to feed. The annual catch of sardines has been reduced by 20 percent. No one yet knows what the amount of ecological damage will be to the eastern Mediterranean.

The silt-free waters of the Nile now flow much more rapidly than the sediment-laden waters of the old river. As a result, parts of the riverbed are being carried away, undermining hundreds of bridges across the river.

In addition, the Aswan High Dam has triggered a variety of health problems. The still waters of Lake Nasser behind the dam are becoming breeding grounds for disease-carrying mosquitoes. The population of *bilharzia*, a parasite carried by water snails, had formerly been limited by the periods of dryness between the annual floods. But there are no longer alternate periods of flood and dryness, and the water snails, which flourish in the constantly placid irrigation canals, are on the increase. As a result, the incidence of *bilharziasis*, a debilitating intestinal disease, has risen to the point that more than half the population is infected.

Although substantial health and economic problems have been generated by the Aswan High Dam, there have been undisputed benefits. The 10,000-MWe capacity of the dam's 12 hydroelectric generators (only a few of which have been placed into service) will provide the electrical power that the Egyptian economy desperately needs. New agricultural lands will be opened by irrigation from the backed-up waters in Lake Nasser, and a new fishing industry will also develop in the lake. But the lake is not filling as rapidly as anticipated, apparently because of unexpected underground losses and a higher evaporation rate than was calculated (due to the neglect of the high wind conditions).

The losses incurred by the construction of the Aswan High Dam will surely be permanent. Will the gains also be permanent or will they turn out to be only temporary? Has too high a price been paid for this new source of energy?

Although the problems associated with the Aswan High Dam are exceptionally severe, they are by no means unique. The construction of any dam alters the downstream ecology as well as that in the lake area behind the dam. What will be the effect of the loss of silt in the downstream portion of the river? How will the silt that builds up behind the dam be removed? Or, if it is not feasible to remove the silt, how long will the facility remain an effective producer of hydroelectric power? What is the value of the land that is submerged by the dam's lake? These and other similar questions must always be answered before intelligent decisions can be reached as to whether to construct a dam and where to locate a dam so that the damage is minimized.

FOSSIL FUELS—MULTIPLE THREATS

Most of the energy that is generated throughout the world at the present time is derived from the burning of fossil fuels—coal, natural gas, and petroleum products. The fact that *combustion* is necessary in the utilization of these fuels presents a number of problems that are different from those encountered with hydroelectric or nuclear reactor power sources in which combustion does not occur.

Because we are using combustible fuels at an ever-increasing rate, and because combustion involves the absorption of oxygen and the production of carbon dioxide, are we not in danger of depleting the world's supply of oxygen and upsetting the oxygen-carbon dioxide balance that is necessary for plant and animal life? There are a multitude of problems associated with the burning of fossil fuels, but, fortunately, this is not one. All of the fossil fuels that have ever been burned have used only 7 out of every 10,000 oxygen molecules available to us. If the burning of these fuels continues at the present accelerating rate (increasing by 5 percent each year), then by the year 2000 we shall have consumed only about 0.2 percent of the available oxygen supply. Even the combustion of all of the world's known reserves of fossil fuels would use less than 3 percent of the available oxygen. Thus, the use of fossil fuels does not present us with the specter of exhausting our oxygen supply.

Figure 7.3 Strip mining—the peeling back of the landscape to reveal the buried seams of coal.

Although we need not be concerned about depleting the atmospheric oxygen, there are numerous environmental problems associated with the utilization of fossil fuels. These problems can be separated into several categories:

1. *Extraction of the Fuel from the Earth.* The most plentiful fuel source in the world is *coal*. The highest quality coal (anthracite) generally occurs sufficiently far underground to require deep-mining techniques. Much of the anthracite in the United States contains so much sulfur that, according to the new air quality standards, it cannot be burned without expensive treatment to remove the sulfur. Moreover, the costs associated with deep-shaft mining have risen to the point that many mines are being closed because they are uneconomical to operate. Consequently, in recent years there has been increased interest in the mining of lower quality but relatively sulfur-free coal that lies close to the surface. *Strip-mining* techniques have been developed which allow the recovery of coal that was once considered to be of little value (Fig. 7.3). Huge machines have been constructed, such as the Consolidation Coal Company's "Gem of Egypt" (Fig. 7.4), which can take 200-ton bites out of the earth to uncover the seams of coal. Strip mining now accounts for almost half of the coal production in the United States.

Figure 7.4 The "Gem of Egypt," the major tool of the Consolidation Coal Company's strip-mining operation in Egypt Valley in Belmont County, Ohio. [Courtesy of Consolidation Coal Company.]

One of the most serious problems associated with the strip mining of coal is the huge amount of land that is torn up in the process. More than 3000 square miles of land (about 2-1/2 times the area of the state of Rhode Island) have been stripped in the United States. It has been estimated that a total of 71,000 square miles in the United States can be profitably stripped. This is an area nearly equal in size to the states of Maryland, New Jersey, New York, and Connecticut combined! Between 4000 and 5000 acres of new land are stripped each week.

The most significant aspect of the land problem is the fact that on only about one-half of the stripped area has there been any attempt at reclamation. Strip-mined land *can* be recovered—at least to a certain degree.

Some mining companies are making efforts to reclaim the stripped land and new laws are forcing others to do so. In Pennsylvania substantial areas of stripped land now accommodate dairy herds. Large tracts of recovered strip-mined land in Illinois are now lush grasslands used mostly for grazing but adaptable for wheat production. Mining statistics from Illinois show that, of 166,000 acres of land affected by strip mining through 1971, 101,000 acres have been reclaimed, primarily as pastureland. But in the more mountainous regions of West Virginia and Kentucky, it is much more difficult to reclaim the land. In many localities sheared-off mountaintops will remain as permanent scars on the landscape. Stripping operators have left behind in Appalachia about 2 million acres of unrestored lands, some 200,000 acres of which are useless "orphan lands," whose owners cannot be found. In the Western states, where there are vast deposits of strip-minable coal, it is claimed that the land can be restored after mining at relatively small cost. More-or-less complete restoration will probably be made a condition of opening up these extensive and valuable coal deposits.

Strip mining affects more than just the land that is mined. Unless careful measures are taken, adjoining property can suffer from landslides, erosion and sedimentation, and deterioration of water quality due to chemical effects. When rain falls on an open strip-mined area, it becomes a giant chemical factory where the exposed iron, magnesium, and sulfates are converted into corrosive compounds that run off into streams and rivers. It has been estimated that strip-mining operations have affected from 3 to 5 times the area that has actually been mined.

Strip mining for coal causes serious and continuing environmental problems. But strip-mined coal appears to be our best hope (perhaps our only hope) to meet the short-term fuel shortage.

The extraction of oil from the ground does not tend to desecrate the land the way that strip mining does. (But the drilling rigs and pumping stations that dot the countryside in many places do not contribute a great deal to the scenery.) The most serious environmental problem associated with oil-well drilling occurs at offshore sites (see Fig. 4.7). Much of the world's oil reserves are located under the continental shelves, off the coasts of North America and Saudi Arabia, in the North Sea, and near the Indonesian islands. Because of the many technical difficulties inherent in offshore drilling, if a rupture occurs or if the drilling opens a crack in the rock that contains the oil deposit, a major leakage of oil into the water can occur before the damage is repaired or the crack is sealed. Leaks of these types have occurred in the Gulf of Mexico and off the coast of Southern California. The release of substantial amounts of oil into the water can be injurious to the marine life and can foul the beaches when the oil washes ashore.

2. *Transportation of the Fuel*. Much of the world's oil is transported to refineries via sea. The tremendous size of modern ocean-going tankers (some are capable of carrying 300,000 tons of oil) has rendered them extremely slow to answer controls. (Consider the momentum of a 300,000-ton tanker traveling at 15 knots! Such a ship requires 2-1/2 miles in which to come to a stop.) The possibility of collision with another ship or with reefs and rocks in narrow waters presents a substantial hazard, as in the case of the *Torrey Canyon* accident in 1967 (Fig. 7.5). When such an accident does occur, rupturing the oil tanks, an enormous oil spill can result, endangering marine life and polluting beaches and harbors.

Leakage from offshore drilling operations and spills from damaged tankers do not represent the major sources of oil pollution in the world's ocean waters. More than two-thirds of the oil dumped into the seas by Man is from the crankcases of automobile and other engines. It has been estimated that as much as 350 million gallons of used crankcase oil is dumped into sewers and eventually runs into the seas each year. Most of this oil could be rerefined and used again, but the practice is not usually followed. Legal restrictions or substantially increased oil prices may force the recycling of oil in the near future.

Figure 7.5 The Torrey Canyon accident in 1967 in which 100,000 gallons of oil were spilled. When this oil washed ashore, it despoiled many miles of English beaches. It was this accident that first focused attention on the problem of oil spills in the ocean waters. [UPI Photo]

Oil is also transported overland via pipelines. In some cases there are serious problems associated with this mode of delivery. The most economical method of transporting oil from the huge fields at Prudhoe Bay on the arctic coast of Alaska is by pipeline to the southern coast of Alaska where the oil is loaded onto tankers for further shipment (see Fig. 7.6). Because the proposed pipeline passes through large areas of untouched land,

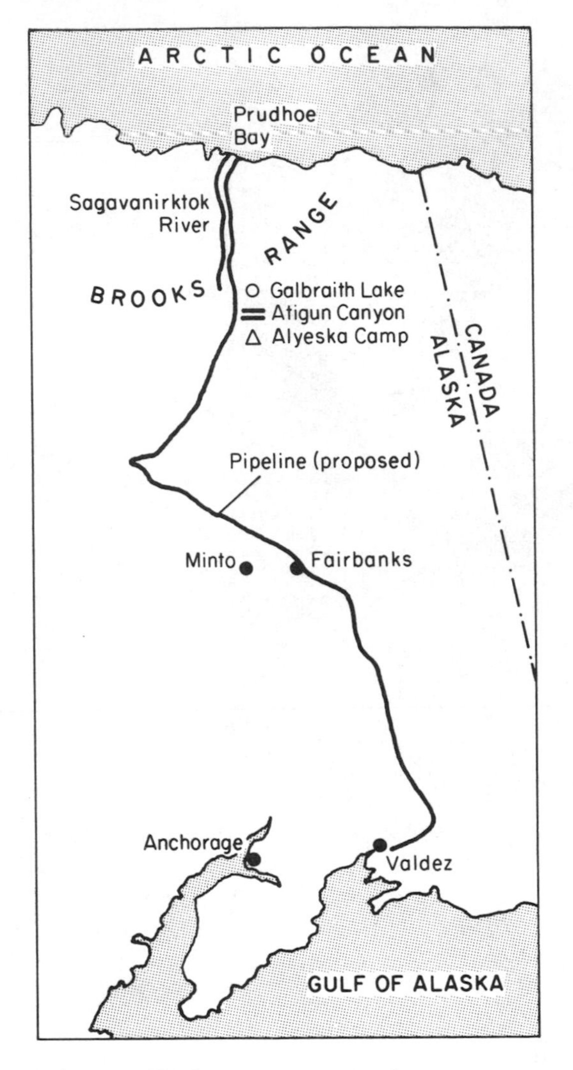

Figure 7.6 Route of the Trans-Alaska Pipeline, now under construction. When completed (in 1980), oil will be pumped from the fields at Prudhoe Bay to the port of Valdez, where it will be loaded onto tankers for transport to refineries.

conservationists fear that the presence of the pipeline will upset the ecological balance of the region. Migratory animals may be forced to use new routes because of blockage by the pipeline. If the line were to break, sizable areas could be soaked by oil before the appropriate valves could be closed. Because the oil must be pumped through the pipeline at high speeds, friction will heat the oil to about 170°F. The hot pipes could conceivably melt their way through the permafrost layer, then sag and rupture. Even if rupture did not occur, the melting of the permafrost might cause irreversible changes in the local ecology. Designers of the system maintain that safety features will eliminate the possibility of catastrophic accidents. We must wait to see what will be the real price of the opening of the Prudhoe Bay oil fields.

Natural gas is also transported via pipeline. In the United States there are almost a quarter of a million miles of underground pipes that deliver natural gas from the sources (primarily in Texas, Louisiana, and Oklahoma) to industrial and urban users. Although this system is relatively trouble free, serious leaks and explosions have occurred on occasions, and several deaths result each year from these incidents.

3. *The Off-Loading of Oil Tankers*. Supertankers now comprise an important segment of the world's tanker fleet; there are now more than 200 of these 1100-ft giants in service. There is no longer any question whether these huge tankers will be involved in the transportation of oil to the United States. The substantial savings in freight costs make the supertanker an economic necessity. The only question is how we will accommodate the ships of the new tanker fleet. No U.S. harbor, with the exception of Puget Sound in the state of Washington (far from the normal tanker lanes), is capable of accommodating the deep-draft supertankers. It is neither economically feasible nor environmentally acceptable to dredge out existing ports and channels so that supertankers can be berthed at the conventional docks. The only alternative

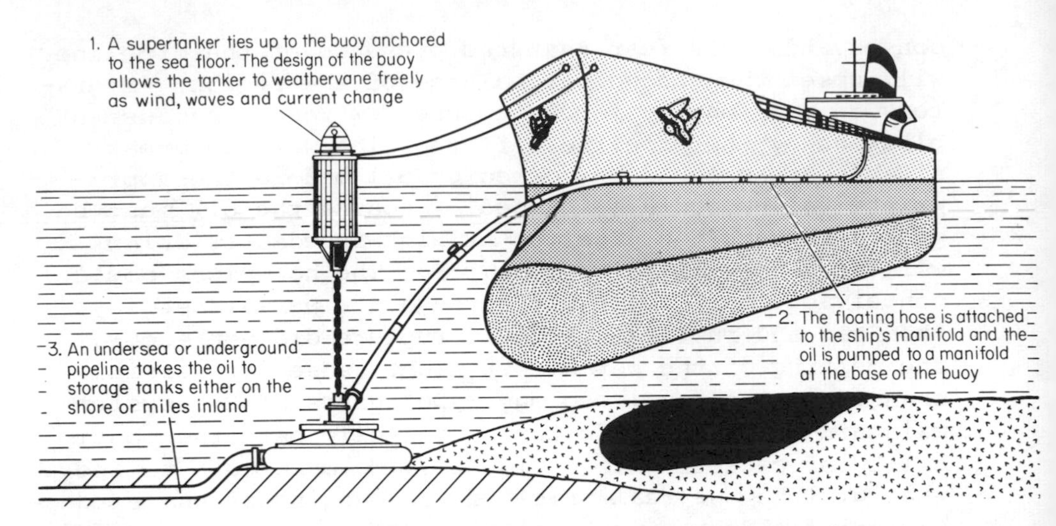

Figure 7.7 A deep-water terminal allows supertankers to load or unload miles from shore. There are over 100 deep-water terminals around the world, but none in the United States. [Exxon]

seems to be to construct deep-water mooring sites several miles offshore and to pump oil from the tankers to onshore facilities through pipelines on the sea floor (Fig. 7.7). Objections to the construction of deep-water tanker ports have been raised on several grounds. Some fear the possibility of oil spills. But studies have shown that the use of offshore terminals will probably result in a far smaller spill effect than if an equal amount of oil were off-loaded from tankers in conventional ports. Of greater importance is the impact on the communities in the neighborhood. When 2 million barrels of oil per day begin flowing from a deep-water terminal to a tank area on shore, this may precipitate a major growth of refineries and petrochemical plants in a region that is not prepared for or cannot accommodate such an industrial complex. Nevertheless, many states, particularly those on the central Gulf Coast, would welcome the new industry that would accompany a deep-water tanker facility. It seems inevitable that at least a few of these offshore tanker terminals will eventually be constructed. But it also seems clear that many policy decisions will have to be made before any site is selected.

4. Combustion of the Fuel. When the fuel has been delivered to the user—coal to steam-generator electrical plants, natural gas to homes, and gasoline to automobiles—the energy content can be utilized only through the combustion process. The burning of fossil fuels releases a variety of noxious gases and particulate matter into the atmosphere (see Table 7.1). The major contributors to this atmospheric pollution are coal and oil products; natural gas is by far the least offensive of the fossil fuels. One of the major problems is the presence of sulfur in coal and oil. Depending on the source, the sulfur content can be several percent and, upon combustion, various oxides of sulfur (particularly SO_2) are produced. The potential for polluting the atmosphere is truly enormous. A 1000-MWe coal-fired power plant burns about 9000 tons of coal each day. If the sulfur content of this coal is 3 percent, 200,000 tons of sulfur dioxide will be released into the air each year—this from only one plant! In addition to the sulfur dioxide, about 40,000 tons of nitrogen oxides will be released, and even if a smoke-cleansing system with 99 percent efficiency is used, 1500 tons of fine particulate matter will escape through the stacks. (Each individual's share is about 3 pounds of soot per year for the electricity he uses.)

TABLE 7.1
Types of Air Pollutants Released by the Combustion of Fossil Fuels

Type	Amount released annually in the U.S. (millions of tons)	Major source
Carbon monoxide	151	Automobiles
Sulfur oxides	33	Power plants
Hydrocarbons	37	Automobiles
Nitrogen oxides	24	Automobiles; power plants
Particulate matter	35	Industrial plants

When SO_2 is released into the atmosphere, it combines with water vapor and forms sulfuric acid. It is this sulfuric acid that is injurious to plant and animal life. Excessive amounts of SO_2 in the atmosphere have been directly linked to the high incidence of several types of respiratory ailments. Recently it has been found that atmospheric sulfuric acid is eating away the limestone facings of many monuments and public buildings in urban areas. The Acropolis in Greece will have to be moved in order to survive the present-day pollution. The Lincoln Memorial in Washington, D.C. is also being attacked and a major project will be required to prevent its surface from decomposing. Restorations expert Kenneth Eisenberg has said with regard to the Lincoln Memorial, "It's like a giant Alka-Seltzer tablet. You can almost hear it fizz when it rains."

The sulfur can be removed from coal and oil, but in many cases a major effort is needed to reduce the content to an acceptable level. In some areas where the sulfur content of the crude oil is particularly high, huge plants have been constructed in order to remove much of the sulfur from the crude oil before it is shipped to the United States for further processing. Stringent regulations have now been placed on the sulfur content of fuels that can be burned in the United States.

Mercury is an extremely poisonous element, and it has recently been discovered that the burning of coal is a significant source of mercury in the atmosphere. It is estimated that 3000 tons of mercury are released into the air annually from coal, about 10 times the amount from natural weathering processes. (Industrially produced mercury wastes amount to about 10,000 tons per year, most of which is eventually discharged into streams and rivers.)

The combustion of natural gas produces far less in the way of pollutants than does either coal or oil. One of the ways of solving the coal and oil problem is to convert these fuels into cleaner-burning gases and liquid hydrocarbons. With the sulfur removed and particulate matter prevented from entering the atmosphere, a primary

Figure 7.8 The Gateway Arch rises above the smog covering downtown St. Louis on November 14, 1966. [Wide World Photos]

source of air pollution would be largely eliminated. As we have already mentioned, a major effort is being mounted to perfect methods for coal gasification and liquefaction. Perhaps within a decade or so we will no longer burn coal but will instead use coal-gas or liquid fuel obtained from coal.

The burning of gasoline in internal combustion engines is the major source of carbon monoxide, nitrogen oxides, and hydrocarbons in the atmosphere (see Table 7.1). In

—— *piceaque gravatum*
Fœdat nube diem[i];

It is this horrid Smoake which obſcures our Church
and makes our Palaces look old, which fouls our Cloth
and corrupts the Waters, ſo as the very Rain, and refre
ing Dews which fall in the ſeveral Seaſons, precipitate t
impure vapour, which, with its black and tenacious qu
lity, ſpots and contaminates whatever is expoſed to it.

—— *Calidoque involvitur undique fumo*[k];

It is this which ſcatters and ſtrews about thoſe black a
ſmutty *Atomes* upon all things where it comes, inſinuati
itſelf into our very ſecret *Cabinets*, and moſt precio
Repoſitories: Finally, it is this which diffuſes and ſpread
Yellowneſſe upon our choyceſt Pictures and Hanging
which does this miſchief at home, is [l] *Avernus* to *Fou*
and kills our *Bees* and *Flowers* abroad, ſuffering nothing
our Gardens to bud, diſplay themſelves, or ripen; ſo

[i] Claud. de rap. Prof. l. i. [k] Ovid.
[l] A lake in Italy, which formerly emitted ſuch noxious fumes, that birds, wh
attempted to fly over it, fell in and were ſuffocated; but it has loſt this bad quality
many ages, and is at preſent well ſtocked with fiſh and fowl.

Figure 7.9 Excerpt from John Evelyn's book, Fumifugium: or The Inconvenience of the Aer and Smoake of London Dissipated, *first published in 1661 and reprinted in 1772. Air pollution has been with us for a long time!*

addition, about 200,000 tons of lead per year are released into the atmosphere from automobile gasolines. It is alarming to note that about 15,000 tons of these various pollutants are introduced into the air *daily* over Los Angeles County. These compounds and the products of the photochemical reactions in which they engage contribute to the noxious mixture known as *smog* (see Fig. 7.8). There seems to be no escape from the health hazards of smog until some effective way is found to remove the pollutants from automobile exhaust gases or until some practical substitute for the internal combustion engine is developed.

ENVIRONMENTAL EFFECTS OF CARBON DIOXIDE AND CARBON MONOXIDE

The production of carbon dioxide is a necessary consequence of every combustion process. Therefore, even if we were to eliminate all of the sulfur from our hydrocarbon fossil fuels and if the combustion of these fuels could be made perfect, we would still release huge quantities of carbon dioxide into the atmosphere. It has been estimated that the carbon dioxide content of the atmosphere has increased by 10 percent in the last 50 years and that by the year 2025 the content will be almost double the value that prevailed in the early nineteenth century before the large-scale use of fossil fuels began.

Carbon dioxide molecules strongly absorb radiant energy of the type emitted from the surface of the Earth. By reradiating this energy at the lower temperature of the upper atmosphere, carbon dioxide reduces the heat energy lost by the Earth to space. (This is called the "greenhouse effect.") Because of this fact, it has been argued that the continued burning of fossil fuels will result in a steady increase in the Earth's surface temperature. Indeed, there was a general increase in temperature between 1860 and 1940; however, since 1940 there has been a slight lowering of temperature for the world as a whole. The problem of atmospheric carbon dioxide is extremely complex, and arguments regarding the inevitability of temperature increases based only on the absorption characteristics of the carbon dioxide molecule are too simplistic. An increase in the temperature of the Earth's surface and lower atmosphere has the compensating effect of increasing evaporation and cloudiness. Because clouds reflect some of the incident sunlight, increases in cloudiness tend to decrease the surface temperature. Furthermore, the release of particulate matter into the atmosphere from fuel burning increases the number of condensation sites around which water droplets can form. The result is an increase in the amount of rain, hail, and thunderstorms which lead to a lowering of the temperature.

The amount of atmospheric carbon dioxide is regulated by the presence of the ocean waters which contain 60 times as much carbon dioxide as does the atmosphere and absorb a large fraction of the carbon dioxide released by the burning of fuels. Also, the increased level of carbon dioxide in the atmosphere actually stimulates the more rapid growth of plants. This increased utilization of carbon dioxide further reduces the atmospheric excess. The carbon dioxide content of plants will eventually be returned to the atmosphere when the plants decompose. But forests account for about one-half of the plant growth in the world and the long lifetime of trees will hold this extra carbon dioxide and distribute its return over a long period of time.

By examining some of the various aspects of the carbon dioxide problem, we see that the world's climate and the world's ecology are influenced to an important extent by changes in the amount of atmospheric carbon dioxide. Apparently, Nature has been kind enough to provide compensatory effects so that our use of fossil fuels will not precipitously alter the climatic features of our world. However, we do not yet completely understand the role that carbon dioxide plays in our environment and we must continue to examine the possible consequences of increased consumption of fossil fuels.

What about carbon monoxide? Are Man's activities, particularly the burning of fossil fuels, provoking a serious imbalance of carbon monoxide in the atmosphere? Apparently not. A recent study shows that about 3.5 billion tons of CO from natural sources enter the atmosphere each year, mostly the result of decaying plant matter. On the other hand, only about 0.27 billion tons of CO are produced by Man. The injection of this amount of excess carbon monoxide into the atmosphere does not yet constitute a serious disturbance of the *average* value. However, in local situations, such as city streets that carry heavy automobile and truck traffic, the carbon monoxide concentration can reach health-affecting levels.

THERMAL POLLUTION

All electric generating plants (except for hydroelectric plants) produce electricity by driving huge turbine generators with steam. The steam is condensed in a cooling system and is cycled back to the heating unit for reuse. The "cooling system" can be water that is pumped from some nearby reservoir (a river, lake, or bay) or it can be a cooling tower in which the heat is dissipated into the atmosphere. Each kilowatt-hour of electric energy generated by a modern fossil fuel plant requires the equivalent of about 1.5 kWh of heat to be rejected at the condenser. Nuclear power plants, because of their lower efficiencies, present thermal pollution problems that are about 50 percent greater. If the heated water is discharged into a flowing river, the effect will be to increase the water temperature by a few degrees in the vicinity of the plant. If the water is discharged into a static reservoir, such as a lake, the effect can be even more severe. In either case, the change in the water temperature will affect the oxygen content of the water and will influence the growth rate of aquatic plants and animals. The ecological balance in the water system will therefore be disturbed to some extent, though in most instances this does not appear to be a major problem.

In order to reduce as far as possible the undesirable effects of heat rejection by power plants, both nuclear and conventional, it will probably become necessary to equip these plants with cooling towers, such as that shown schematically in Fig. 5.12. (Several of the newer plants are so equipped; see Fig. 5.13.) By dissipating most of the excess heat into the atmosphere instead of the water system, the damage to the aquatic life will be considerably lessened. But the use of cooling towers will mean a more expensive operation and it will also mean a change in the local atmospheric conditions (for example, an increase in fog formation). Although either system tends to alter the natural conditions, on balance it often seems preferable to reject as much of the heat as possible into the atmosphere instead of into rivers, lakes, and bays.

Thermal pollution is generated by the energy *user* as well as by the energy *producer*. Almost all of the energy we use is eventually converted into heat, by friction, by electrical resistance heating, and in combustion processes. Most of this waste heat is dissipated into the air where it contributes to the general atmospheric heating. In large cities, where energy consumption is concentrated, the air temperature is usually several degrees higher than in the surrounding rural areas. (Washington, D.C. has 30 more frost-free days per year than the surrounding areas.) This increased temperature is also an important factor in the production of urban smog.

In order to gauge the magnitude of the urban waste heat problem, consider the situation in Los Angeles County. The population of the county is approximately 7 million people. Assuming an average rate of energy use of 10 kW per person (which is the national average), the total for the county is 7×10^{10} W. The area of Los Angeles County is 4069 square miles or approximately 10^{10} m^2. Therefore, the average rate of energy usage (and hence heat production) is about 7 W/m^2. Solar radiation reaching the surface of the Earth, averaged over a day, is about 200 W/m^2. Thus the artificially produced heat in this urban area is about 3 percent of that received from the Sun, and this figure will increase substantially as the rate of energy usage continues to climb. It has been estimated that by the year 2000, the rate of release of thermal energy by the 56 million people who will then live in the Boston-Washington corridor will be about 32 W/m^2, a significant fraction of the solar energy input.

Even if we discover ways to eliminate the other problems associated with energy production and usage, thermal pollution will still be with us. And we do not know what the long-term consequences of this subtle form of pollution will be.

QUESTIONS AND EXERCISES

1. The construction of the Glen Canyon Dam on the Colorado River in a remote section of northern Arizona has flooded 200,000 acres of canyon lands. Conservationists strongly objected to this destruction of natural canyons. But the dam has formed 200-mile-long Lake Powell and now visitors may tour the partially submerged canyons by boat. Whereas previously only very few persons ever saw the original canyons, thousands now see the lake region every year. Comment on whether the environmental price paid for the Glen Canyon Dam was too high.

2. There are approximately 300,000 miles of overhead high-voltage electrical transmission lines in service in the United States. The rights-of-way on which the familiar steel towers are placed average 110 feet in width. How much land is used for these transmission lines? Compare this area with that of the state of Connecticut.

3. The EPA has estimated the annual cost of air pollution damage to health, vegetation, and property values to be more than $16 billion. How much does air pollution cost *you* each year?

4. It has been estimated that 71,000 square miles of the United States could be profitably strip mined. Suppose that, instead of strip mining, this area were covered with some kind of solar energy system that would absorb 10 percent of the energy in sunlight and transform it into electricity. Compute the amount of energy that such a system would produce annually and compare the figure with the present worldwide rate of energy consumption. (Would 71,000 square miles of recovered strip-mined land have any less visual appeal than 71,000 square miles of solar cells?)

5. Approximately one-half of the total U.S. electrical generating capacity (460,000 MWe) uses coal as fuel. A 1000-MWe plant requires about 9000 tons of coal per

day. How many cubic feet is this? (The density of coal is approximately 90 lb/ft^3.) If a near-surface coal seam is 10-ft thick, how many acres must be stripped per day to supply the coal needed to produce electricity in the United States? (1 acre = 43,560 ft^2.) Make any comments that seem appropriate.

Chapter 8
OUTLINE FOR THE FUTURE

Although an impending crisis in energy has been visible to many observers for several years, only in 1973 was the general public made painfully aware of the severity of the situation. The problem was heightened by the impact of the embargo on the shipment of oil from the Arab countries, and the President called for a program to make the United States self-sufficient in energy resources by 1980. How can we accomplish this goal? How will we meet the energy challenge in 1980 and in the next century? The various segments of the problem can be divided into categories depending on the time intervals required for the different developments. A possible sequence of events can be sketched in the following way.

THE SHORT TERM (1975-1976)

In any human activity as huge and as scattered as is the gigantic energy industry, substantial changes are slow to occur. As a case in point, consider nuclear power. Although the first commercial nuclear power plant began operating in 1957, only about 1 percent of the total U.S. energy consumption in 1973 was derived from nuclear reactors. The primary reason for the slow development of nuclear power has been the enormous series of technological problems that are associated with the introduction of a new and highly complex industry. The same will be true of the development of solar power, the recovery of shale oil, and the construction of fusion reactors. There is necessarily a long delay between the time that the operating principles are established or the first pilot plant is built and the time that the new system becomes a significant factor in the overall energy picture. Therefore, on a short time scale we can hope to accomplish only limited objectives of a more-or-less emergency nature. These include:

· Various energy economies can be instituted by voluntary actions or by regulation. The amount of gasoline used can be reduced by lowered speed limits or by rationing. Heating oil can be conserved by lowering the average temperature maintained in homes and businesses. (It has been estimated that a reduction in temperature by 5°F will lower the consumption of heating fuels by 15 percent.)

· The burden on oil supplies can be reduced by reconverting to coal those electrical generating plants that recently changed to oil as their fuel.

· Air quality standards can be temporarily suspended in emergency situations in order to allow the burning of coal with higher sulfur content than now permitted. The introduction of emission controls on automobile exhaust fumes can be delayed. (This will result in the more efficient operation of automobile engines.) Both of these measures save fuel at the cost of lowering air quality.

THE NEAR INTERMEDIATE TERM (TO 1980)

· Energy economies can be continued and expanded during this period. New home construction can be required to include better insulation so that heating and cooling require less fuel. Increased emphasis can be placed on the use of railroads for intercity transport of goods. (The movement of goods by truck uses about 4 times as much fuel as does movement by rail.)

· By 1977 the Trans-Alaskan Pipeline should be open and delivering 600,000 barrels of oil per day. By 1980 the capacity should be 2 million barrels of oil and 10 trillion cubic feet of gas per day, a significant fraction of the U.S. oil and gas consumption. (For comparison, before the oil embargo, the United States imported about 1 million barrels of oil per day from Arab countries.)

· The production and use of coal—particularly, strip-mined coal—can be significantly increased, relieving some of the drain on oil supplies. The use of oil for the generation of electricity can be almost completely eliminated.

· The search for and development of offshore deposits of oil and natural gas can be speeded up.

· Increased production of oil from the Canadian tar sands can be realized.

· The nuclear reactor program can be stepped up. The approximately 10-year period for planning, licensing, and construction now required could be reduced to about 5 years.

It is the announced aim of the U.S. government that this country become self-sufficient in energy by 1980. The Federal Energy Office (FEO) has developed a schedule for the expansion of our various energy sources to meet this goal. These figures, in which all of the sources are given in units of millions of barrels of oil equivalent per day, are shown in Table 8.1. Whether or not we can actually achieve this ambitious schedule of resource development remains to be seen. Most experts, however, are skeptical that complete self-sufficiency can be attained on this short time scale.

TABLE 8.1
Federal Energy Office Schedule of Resource Development to Achieve Energy Self-Sufficiency by 1980[a]

	1973	1974	1975	1976	1977	1978	1979	*1980*
Oil	*10.9*	11.1	11.3	11.6	12.0	12.5	13.0	*14.0*
Shale	-	-	-	-	-	0.1	0.3	*0.5*
Natural gas	*11.2*	11.2	11.3	11.5	11.8	12.0	12.8	*13.2*
Coal	*6.9*	7.4	7.9	8.4	9.0	9.6	10.3	*11.0*
Hydro	*1.4*	1.4	1.4	1.4	1.4	1.5	1.5	*1.5*
Nuclear	*0.1*	0.2	0.4	0.4	0.6	0.8	0.9	*1.3*
Geothermal	-	-	-	-	-	0.1	0.3	*0.6*
Total supply	*30.5*	31.3	32.3	33.3	34.8	36.6	39.1	*42.1*
Demand @ 2 percent	*36.6*	37.3	38.0	38.8	39.6	40.4	41.2	*42.1*
Net imports needed	*6.1*	6.0	5.7	5.5	4.8	3.8	2.1	*0*

[a]All figures in millions of barrels per day of oil equivalent

THE INTERMEDIATE TERM (TO 1990)

- Energy economies should be continued. Increased use of mass transit systems could reduce the demand for oil in transportation.

- The program to develop breeder reactors should see a number of power plants of this type in service with many more in various stages of construction.

- Coal gasification and liquefaction plants should be producing significant quantities of petroleum-substitute fuels.

- Methods for the recovery of oil from shale deposits should be developed and some plants put in operation.

• The utilization of solar and geothermal energy should be beginning. An appreciable fraction of new construction should include solar heating and cooling systems.

THE LONG TERM (TO 2020 OR 2050)

• In this period the widespread use of power generated by fusion reactions should begin.

• The use of solar and geothermal power should also be extensive.

• The reserves of oil and natural gas may be very nearly depleted by the middle of the twenty-first century. Almost all of the liquid fuels and raw materials for the petrochemical industry will be produced from coal.

The time schedule for the various developments listed above is predicated on reasonable expectations for technological advances. We know that oil can be extracted from tar sands and from shale. We know how to explore for and how to recover offshore oil. We know how to gasify and to liquefy coal. Bringing these sources of energy "on-line" in significant quantities seems to be largely a matter of seriously setting out to do so. It seems reasonable to expect that these new sources of chemical fuels can be developed and that the nuclear power industry can be expanded to meet our energy needs during the next few decades. However, we may experience shortages during this period, and if unexpected difficulties arise, we may have significant and unpleasant shortfalls in energy supplies. It seems certain that energy usage will become more and more expensive throughout this period. And it seems likely that the quality of our environment will suffer somewhat in the process—hopefully, not too much.

The situation with regard to power from fusion, solar, and geothermal sources is less predictable. Completely new technologies must be developed to exploit these sources. Perhaps we will be fortunate and the various problems will be solved before the end of this century.

But it seems more reasonable that we will be forced to rely on chemical fuels and fission power for the next 50 to 75 years. The prospect is that only strip-mined coal and breeder reactors will see us through our years of difficulty.

In summary, this seems to be the situation that we are facing: For the next few years we will probably experience a general shortage of energy, sometimes severe. By 1980 conditions should start to improve as long-lead-time developments begin to relieve the shortages. Even so, during the 1980s the balance may still be precarious. Real progress should be manifest by about 1990 as breeder reactors and coal-based liquid and gaseous fuels come into general use. Although we may have adequate energy supplies during this period, energy will be expensive and there will still be considerable environmental problems. Probably not before 2020 will we see the general availability of clean, inexpensive energy, and this new era might not begin until 2050.

The world will probably survive the "energy crisis" (perhaps with only inconveniences and not with near catastrophe), and some of us may live to see the day of plentiful energy supplies. But this day will not come quickly, nor cheaply, nor without a considerable struggle. In the long term, we are not really limited by energy supplies—the potential at our disposal is truly enormous. Instead, the ultimate limitation is the degree to which we can safely alter our environment. This will be our main long-range problem.

QUESTIONS AND EXERCISES

1. List some of the situations that you see every day in which energy is used wastefully. How many of these offer real possibilities for energy economies?

2. What kinds of problems might develop that could delay the projections for 1980 and 1990?

3. If energy were actually available in almost unlimited quantities and at very little cost, what kinds of changes might this make in everyday life?

4. It has been said that, given enough energy, we could live off of dirt. What does this statement mean?

Appendix

POWERS-OF-TEN NOTATION

In order to write large and small numbers (such as 40,000,000,000 and 0.000 000 003) in a compact way, we use the *powers-of-ten* notation. For example,

$$10 \times 10 = 100 = 10^2$$

$$10 \times 10 \times 10 = 1000 = 10^3$$

$$10 \times 10 \times 10 \times 10 = 10{,}000 = 10^4$$

That is, the number of times that 10 is multiplied together appears in the result as the superscript of 10 (called the *exponent* of 10 or the *power* to which 10 is raised).

Any number can be expressed in powers-of-ten notation. For example,

$$147{,}000{,}000 = 1.47 \times 100{,}000{,}000 = 1.47 \times 10^8$$

Products of powers of 10 are expressed as

$$10^2 \times 10^3 = (10 \times 10) \times (10 \times 10 \times 10) = 10^5 = 10^{(2+3)}$$

That is, in general, the product of 10^n and 10^m is $10^{(n+m)}$:

$$10^n \times 10^m = 10^{(n+m)}$$

If the power of 10 appears in the denominator, the exponent is given a negative sign:

$$\frac{1}{10} = 0.1 = 10^{-1}$$

$$\frac{1}{100} = 0.01 = 10^{-2}$$

$$\frac{1}{1000} = 0.001 = 10^{-3}$$

In general,

$$\frac{1}{10^m} = 10^{-m}$$

Any decimal number can be expressed as a negative power of 10:

$$0.037 = \frac{37}{1000} = \frac{3.7}{100} = 3.7 \times 10^{-2}$$

Notice that in going from 0.037 to 3.7, we move the decimal *two* places to the right; therefore, the exponent of 10 that appears in the result is -2.

Calculations involving large or small numbers are made considerably easier by using the powers-of-ten notation:

$$\frac{640,000}{4,000,000,000} = \frac{6.4 \times 10^5}{4 \times 10^9} = \frac{6.4}{4} \times 10^{(5-9)} = 1.6 \times 10^{-4}$$

Sometimes we use a prefix to a unit to express the appropriate unit. For example, *centi-* means 1/100; therefore, *centimeter* means 1/100 of a meter. Other commonly used prefixes are

k = kilo- = 10^3	m = milli- = 10^{-3}
M = mega- = 10^6	μ = micro- = 10^{-6}
G = giga- = 10^9	n = nano- = 10^{-9}

SUGGESTIONS FOR FURTHER READING

The literature on energy and energy problems has mushroomed in recent years and the amount of material is now truly enormous. This list gives only a few references which the reader may find informative. For a comprehensive survey of sources available up to early 1972, see R. H. Romer, *American Journal of Physics Vol. 40,* p. 805, 1972. Some of the more recent books are

Nuclear Power and the Public, H. Foreman, ed., Doubleday, Garden City, New York, 1972.

The Energy Crisis, L. Rocks and R. P. Runyon, Crown, New York, 1972.

United States Energy through the Year 2000, W. G. Dupree and J. A. West, U.S. Govt. Printing Office, Washington, D.C., 1972.

Nuclear Energy: Its Physics and Its Social Challenge, D. R. Inglis, Addison-Wesley, Reading, Massachusetts, 1973.

Energy and the Future, A. Hammond, W. Metz, and T. Maugh, American Association for the Advancement of Science, Washington, D.C., 1973.

The Logarithmic Century, R. E. Lapp, Prentice-Hall, Englewood Cliffs, New Jersey, 1973.

Problems of Our Physical Environment, J. Priest, Addison-Wesley, Reading, Massachusetts, 1973.

Energy Crisis in Perspective, J. C. Fisher, Wiley, New York, 1974.

Energy, Electric Power, and Man, T. J. Healy, Boyd and Fraser, San Francisco, 1974.

INDEX